TEACH YOURSELF BOOKS

Music

King Palmer
Associate of the Royal Academy of Music

NTC Publishing Group

Long-renowned as *the* authoritative source for self-guided
learning – with more than 30 million copies sold worldwide –
the *Teach Yourself* series includes over 200 titles in the fields
of languages, crafts, hobbies, sports, and other leisure activities.

This edition was first published in 1992 by NTC Publishing Group,
4255 West Touhy Avenue, Lincolnwood (Chicago), Illinois 60646 –
1975 U.S.A. Originally published by Hodder and Stoughton Ltd.
Copyright 1978, 1986, 1992 by King Palmer.

Printed in England by Clays Ltd, St Ives plc.

CONTENTS

CONTENTS

— ABOUT THIS BOOK —

This book has four objectives:

1 To explore the possibilities of playing a musical instrument or singing, with or without the help of a teacher. Chapter 1 gives a broad survey of instruments and voices, and discusses the techniques involved, the relative cost and difficulty of different instruments, expectations of progress, etc. Instruments suitable for children are considered, also how to make the most of the many opportunities of making music. Chapters 4 to 7 give detailed descriptions of different instruments and voices. Chapter 3 gives advice on practising.

2 To provide a first introduction to the full range of syllabus topics, practical and historical, which are required for the average school music examination, with guidance when study in greater depth is required; also a clear overview of these subjects for the general reader who wishes to enhance his or her musical knowledge.

Chapters 4 to 13 discuss these topics, and self-testing questions and answers are provided. These chapters will also be useful to candidates for Teaching Diplomas in music (paperwork for LRSM, ARCM, etc.).

3 To provide a detailed study of the theory of music which is necessary for the pursuit of practical music, with self-testing questions and

answers. Chapters 2, 6, 7 and 9 provide preparation for Grade Five Theory examinations (Associated Board of the Royal Schools of Music, etc.), which candidates must pass before taking practical examinations from Grade Six onwards.

4   To provide reference sections, including a Glossary of Musical Terms, and a checklist of composers classified according to different periods of musical history.

'He' has been used throughout this book where a neutral between sexes pronoun is required. However, it should be noted that 'he' is intended to be fully interchangeable with 'she'.

1
THE PURSUIT OF MUSIC

In recent years there has been a great upsurge of interest in making music. People of all ages are discovering that there can be great satisfaction in learning to play or sing, and that in a world where stress has become the 'modern sickness', music can provide relaxation.

Assuming that you have a real desire to make some kind of music, you have then to consider which instrument might be the most suitable (or whether you would prefer to sing). This chapter explores the different possibilities.

Singing

There are many opportunities for anyone who has a reasonable singing voice, trained or untrained. Church choirs, choral societies, chamber choirs, operatic societies, carol parties, and many other singing groups give men and women (and boys and girls) the opportunity of making music together, and foster the spirit of working as a team.

The ability to read music is, of course, very desirable, but not always essential. And if the vocal organs are normal and healthy much can be done to develop the volume, compass and quality of the voice. Singing is also an excellent way of improving the speaking voice.

The singer who has sufficient skill to become a soloist will be greatly in demand as an amateur performer. He is recommended, wherever possible, to learn to play the piano at least well enough to accompany himself, for this will add much to his personal pleasure and performing ability.

Apart from membership of local choirs and operatic societies, there are opportunities to take part in performances of Handel's *Messiah* and other works from 'scratch' (i.e. after a single rehearsal). There are also weekend courses in choral singing at residential adult education colleges.

—— Learning to play an instrument ——

The concert artist who plays the piano, violin or other instrument must have inborn talent, dedication leading to years of unremitting practice, and an ample measure of good health and good fortune.

Though the average person can scarcely hope to reach such a pinnacle, he should be able to acquire sufficient skill on an instrument to bring him pleasure and satisfaction (the average person is seldom tone deaf, or entirely lacking in rhythmic feeling and response).

In seeking the most suitable instrument, however, there are a number of considerations which should be taken into account.

1 Are you willing to take lessons, which may be costly and extend over several years, or do you wish to try to teach yourself with the aid of a tutor, after taking a few lessons? With most instruments, help from a teacher is needed if real progress is to be made, but there are some you could learn by yourself.
2 How useful is the instrument likely to be – would you rather play on your own, or with others in an orchestra or band? If the latter, how portable is the instrument?
3 How much practice are you prepared to do? Progress on some instruments is likely to be quicker than on others, but some regular practice is essential.
4 What is the instrument likely to cost? Is it possible to borrow or hire an instrument?
5 Do you have the time and place to practise undisturbed, and without disturbing anyone else?

——————— **Learning by yourself** ———————

It is possible to attain some degree of skill on certain instruments without the help of a teacher. These are dealt with below.

The piano

1 Playing the piano by ear. Some people have a natural talent for reproducing popular songs and the simpler classics (with varying degrees of accuracy) which they have heard performed.
2 Playing from a printed melody, and improvising an accompaniment from chord symbols; this involves some knowledge of musical notation. There is a chapter on improvisation in *Teach Yourself the Piano* (Hodder & Stoughton).

The recorder

This end-blown flute is easy to blow, and it is not difficult to learn to play simple tunes from a book, although advanced playing requires considerable skill and practice, and some help from a teacher.

The harmonica (mouth organ)

A reasonable degree of skill can be acquired on this 'suck-and-blow' instrument, and some players (e.g. Larry Adler, b.1914) have achieved remarkable virtuosity.

The tin whistle

This simple end-blown pipe is easy to blow and finger, though it is less popular than the recorder.

Small electronic keyboards

Small electronic keyboards, which usually have small keys and a limited compass, can be played by children or adults with little knowledge of conventional musical notation, since there are usually devices which automatically 'programme' chords in different keys, as well as in various rhythms.

The chromaharp

This is a form of autoharp, and is provided with buttons which, when pressed, add complete chords to melody notes. The number of chords varies from five to twenty-seven, according to the size of the instrument. The chromaharp is easy to tune and play, and is useful for accompanying simple tunes like folk songs and nursery rhymes.

——— Learning from a teacher ———

To become a reasonable performer on most instruments it is usually necessary to take lessons from a teacher. The choice of a suitable teacher needs to be made with care – some are better qualified to teach than others, whether by the possession of a teaching diploma or by wide experience. Personal recommendation is often valuable, and there is also a *Professional Register of Private Teachers of Music* (published by the Incorporated Society of Musicians) which lists approved teachers in all districts, and is available for reference in public libraries and music shops.

Some pupils may wish to take 'grade' examinations in music, which can provide a stimulus for regular practice and a yardstick for measuring progress. These are held three times a year at local centres throughout the United Kingdom, and about once a year in most parts of the British Commonwealth, Egypt, South Africa, etc. The principal examining bodies are the Associated Board of the Royal Schools of Music (Royal Academy of Music, Royal College of Music, Royal Northern College of Music, and Royal Scottish Academy of Music and Drama), Guildhall School of Music and Drama, Trinity College of Music, and London College of Music. Details may be obtained from most music shops, and addresses of examining bodies will be found in *The British Music*

Yearbook (published annually by Rhinegold Publishing Ltd) which is in most public libraries. The examinations, in practical subjects and the theory of music, are usually in eight grades, and a beginner might expect to be able to take Grade One in about a year. The usual requirements for practical subjects include the satisfactory performance of three pieces, scales, sight-reading, and aural tests.

In the USA, examinations are organised by a number of Schools of Music, of which local music dealers will be able to supply details. In Canada the Royal Conservatory of Music (University of Toronto) organises music examinations in ten grades. Trinity College of Music also holds examinations in the USA and Canada.

— Choosing an instrument to learn —

The piano

The *piano* is the most popular of all instruments. It is especially suitable for home music-making, since the music which it produces is complete and satisfying in itself. In the very early stages it is easier to play than some other instruments. The string player, for example, has to make notes and may therefore play out of tune. The pianist is not concerned with good intonation (i.e. playing in tune), as notes are ready made and cannot be played out of tune unless, of course, the piano itself is out of tune. Nevertheless, the pianist should have a good musical ear, otherwise the playing is likely to be mechanical; but the violinist with a faulty ear will be able to make even less progress. The chief problem for the beginner is that of co-ordinating the two hands, and this may take some time to overcome.

Early instruments

Although there has been a revival of interest in early keyboard instruments such as the *harpischord, clavichord* and *spinet* (as well as in early string and wind instruments – *viols, lutes, baroque flutes* and *oboes*, etc.), this is a specialised field of study, and teachers are not always readily available.

The violin

Apart from its expressive beauty as a solo instrument, the *violin* leads the string quartet, and is the most important instrument in the orchestra. The main problems of violin playing are intonation and the acquisition of a fine tone (i.e. fine quality of sound). Perfect control of the bow and of the fingers of the left hand can be attained only by practice and experience. In all matters of tone the ear plays an important part, and the performer himself must be his severest critic.

Other stringed instruments

The technique of the violin applies, to a large extent, to the viola and cello, and the standard of difficulty is about the same. The *viola* is simply a large violin with a less brilliant but richer tone. Its slight disability is that it is too small in relation to its pitch (i.e. compass of notes), and though invaluable in the orchestra and string quartet, it is less useful as a solo instrument.

The *cello* has a full, rich tone, and in the orchestra it is often given solo passages of characteristic beauty. Its size and weight, however, may present problems if it has to be taken on public transport.

The *double bass*, the deepest voiced member of the string family, is primarily an orchestral instrument, and is easier to play than the violin or the cello, but because of its size and weight, and the fact that it cannot be used to play solos in the home, it is unlikely to be considered as a possible choice.

The *guitar* is a most useful instrument for accompanying the voice, and although guitar music is normally written in music notation, it is possible to learn to play simple accompaniments, suitable for popular and folk tunes, by means of 'chord symbols' and diagrams which show where the fingers are to be placed. Solo classical guitar playing is a very different matter and requires much skill and serious study. Several kinds of electrically amplified guitars are used in pop groups.

In recent years there has been some revival of interest in the *banjo*, an American Negro instrument with from five to nine strings, and the *mandolin*, of Neapolitan origin with four double strings, which can sometimes be electrically amplified.

Wind instruments

The finger technique of wind instruments is less difficult than that of the piano or violin, but the use of lips, teeth, tongue and breath must be considered. Certain physical disabilities may complicate the playing of wind instruments – missing or irregular teeth may make tone production difficult and respiratory troubles may prevent proper control of the breath. Wind instruments can be divided into two groups: woodwind and brass. This classification is not strictly accurate, for sometimes wood-wind instruments are made of metal, and brass instruments of other metals.

Woodwind instruments   There are four families of instruments in the woodwind group: *flute, oboe, clarinet* and *bassoon*. There are also additional instruments: *piccolo* (small flute), *cor anglais* or *English horn* (large oboe), *bass clarinet* (large clarinet), and *double bassoon* (large bassoon). The flute, oboe and clarinet are all about the same length, between 60 and 67.5 cm (2 ft–2 ft 3 ins); the piccolo measures about 30 cm (1 ft), and the bassoon about 1.5 m (5 ft). Of these instruments the flute and the clarinet are probably the easiest to play.

The sound of all wind instruments is produced by making a column of air vibrate in a tube. This is done in several ways. The flautist blows across a small hole at one end of the flute. The clarinettist has a mouthpiece to which a flat piece of cane, called a reed, is fastened in order to leave a small gap. The oboe and bassoon player's mouthpiece consists of two small pieces of cane bound together with a gap in between; this is called a double reed. The breath must be passed through it slowly and evenly, and the control required to do this makes the oboe and the bassoon two of the most difficult woodwind instruments to play.

The *saxophone,* found most frequently in the dance or light orchestra and the military band, has been used on occasions in the symphony orchestra (e.g. Bizet, *L'Arlésienne* Suites (1872); Vaughan Williams, *Job* (1930), Symphony No 9 (1958); Ravel, *Bolero* (1928). Though made of metal, the saxophone has a reed and mouthpiece similar to those of the clarinet.

The *recorder* is now widely used as an educational instrument, and it is also very suitable for amateur music-making, especially in the home. The smaller recorders are not expensive, and the repertoire, for solo re-corder and keyboard instrument, a 'consort' of several recorders, or recorders combined with string instruments, includes some very attractive music. There are also jazz and rock 'n' roll recorder albums, with guitar accompaniment.

Brass instruments   The group of brass instruments in the orchestra consists of the *French horn, trumpet, trombone* and *tuba*. The *cornet*, which is mainly used in brass and military bands though occasionally in the orchestra, is similar to the trumpet but is shorter, has a mellower tone and is rather easier to play. Other brass instruments, such as the *flügel horn* and the *euphonium*, are also mainly used in brass and military bands. The tone of all brass instruments is produced by the action of the player's lips, which take the place of reeds. The French horn, which has a coiled tube about 6 m (12 ft) long and a narrow bore, is the most difficult to play. The trumpet and trombone in the dance orchestra have a style of playing quite different from that normally used in the symphony orchestra. The tuba is a large, unwieldy instrument with a deep, powerful tone.

Percussion instruments

The *timpani* (*kettledrums*), which are the only drums capable of producing sounds of definite pitch, were almost the only percussion instruments used by the early classical composers. The timpanist needs to acquire considerable skill, and the professional player may be called upon to handle up to four pedal-tuned timpani. The amateur timpanist may only have the less costly hand-tuned instruments at his disposal.

Modern composers use a wide variety of percussion instruments – *side drum, bass drum, cymbals, triangle, tambourine, castanets, gong, tubular bells, glockenspiel, xylophone* and *vibraphone*, etc. The technique varies considerably from instrument to instrument, and further details will be found in Chapter 7. Some percussion instruments (e.g. *xylophone*) require a high degree of skill; others (e.g. *triangle, maracas*) can be played by almost anyone with a good sense of rhythm, and the ability to count bars of music. Although the timpanist normally just remains in charge of his drums, several of the other percussion instruments may be played by the same player, if they are used one at a time.

Fig. 1
Evelyn Glennie, percussion player. Profoundly deaf by the age of 12, she has
become an international soloist.

The harp

The *harp*, which was once found in Victorian drawing rooms, is now mainly used in the orchestra, and in smaller ensembles. It requires considerable skill, and a suitable teacher may not be easy to find.

Tuning the harp is quite a lengthy process, and transport may not be easy to arrange; also the cost of the instrument is likely to be high.

The organ family

The electronic organ   *Electronic organs* vary in size from small, single-manual organs to large organs with two or three manuals,* full-size pedal-board for the feet, and a reverberation system designed to reproduce the acoustics of a large church or concert hall. These large organs require as much skill as a pipe organ (see page 77).

The pipe organ   A *pipe organ* with two or more manuals and a pedal-board is by no means easy to play. In addition to the pianist's problems of co-ordinating two hands, the organist has to co-ordinate both the feet and the hands. Another difficulty may be that opportunities for practice will be limited, for it is hardly practicable to install a pipe organ in the average house, although an electronic organ may be a useful substitute. However, it may be possible to arrange to use the organ of a local church for a few hours a week, in return for a contribution to church funds.

The technique of the pipe organ differs, in many respects, from that of the piano, but the two instruments have a good deal in common, and it may be an advantage to study the piano for a while before proceeding to the organ since the beginner will have many practical difficulties to contend with – stops, different manuals, the pedal-board, registration,† etc.

The fundamental differences between piano and organ technique are:

1   If the pianist depresses a key while holding down the sustaining pedal the sound will continue until it finally fades, even if the hand is lifted

---

* Manual (Lat. *manus*, hand) = keyboard, especially on the organ or harpsichord.

† Organ stops control the wind supply to a *register*, or set, of pipes. *Registration* is the art of selection and combining stops.

from the keyboard. On the organ a sound is sustained only so long as a key is held down; it does not fade, but if the key is released it ceases instantly.

2 The pianist can produce different levels of sound by depressing the piano keys in different ways; but however the organ keys are depressed the sound will be the same. The organist can increase or diminish the sound by other methods, such as opening and closing a box-like contrivance called the 'swell'.

3 The piano has only one keyboard. The organ normally has two, three or more manuals. A group of organ pipes is linked to each manual, and the pipes are divided into sets, each set producing a different kind of tone-colour. By manipulating knobs or levers called 'stops', the organist is able to use any set of pipes on its own, or several sets in combination.

4 The pedals of a piano are used to sustain or soften sounds. The organ pedals form an additional keyboard which is played with the feet, and which produces bass notes.

The reed organ family   Although reed organs are not common nowadays, either the *harmonium* or the *American organ* (which are rather similar in general construction) could serve as a useful preliminary to pipe organ playing. Reed organs are, in general, easier to play than pipe organs, the wind usually being supplied by treadles worked by the feet. In addition there is only a limited number of stops.

The piano-accordion

The *piano-accordion* consists of pleated bellows, with piano-type keys for the right hand, and buttons for the left hand which produce bass notes and simple chords. The piano-accordion is one of the easier instruments to play, with some help from a teacher, and is popular as a solo instrument, for accompanying vocal and folk groups, and for taking part in accordion bands.

───────── Music for children ─────────

The earliest age at which music lessons may usually begin for the average child, as opposed to the child with exceptional talent, depends on aptitude and on the instrument chosen. A child may show evident signs of pleasure when listening to music, and may be able to whistle tunes he has heard or pick them out on the piano. Though it is not possible to lay down hard and fast rules, it may be useful to give approximate ages at which a musical child may study different instruments.

A child of four, or even younger, may be shown how to pick out notes and melodies on the piano and encouraged to do so himself, but until he is able to read words fluently it is likely that he will play music chiefly by rote (i.e. by remembering the sounds without reading the notes). For the normal child, therefore, regular lessons should not begin until the age of six, and then only if he shows a positive interest. On the other hand, a musical parent who is willing to take some part in the child's practice, and perhaps to play duets with him, may further his enjoyment and progress.

Lessons on the violin or cello can usually be begun at six or seven, as these instruments are made in several sizes to suit children of different ages. The Japanese Suzuki system teaches children by rote, in groups, from about three years of age, using tiny violins and cellos. The viola, being heavier than the violin, is more fatiguing to hold up, and the fingers must be stretched wider; but younger children sometimes start with a violin fitted with thicker strings. The full-size double bass needs height and strength, but there are smaller 'mini-basses' which can be played by younger children.

Of the orchestral woodwind instruments, the flute and clarinet are probably the easiest to learn, and lessons may be begun about nine years of age or younger, depending on aptitude. The oboe, which is more difficult for a child to play, may be studied at about the same age, but the bassoon, a heavy instrument requiring a good deal of wind, should not usually be begun until about twelve.

A child of eight with a normal constitution could begin to study the cornet or trumpet. Work on the French horn, saxophone or trombone should begin rather later. Practice on brass instruments is fatiguing for the beginner, and should be limited to a few minutes at a time to begin with.

It is usually advisable to delay the study of the pipe or the larger electronic organs until some progress has been made on the piano. A child who wishes to play the pipe organ should be able to reach the pedals comfortably. Most young children find pleasure in learning the recorder. Practice periods need not be long, and early progress should be rapid enough to sustain interest. The recorder is useful for both home and school activities. There is also an '*Aulos*' side-blown fife, which provides a good introduction to the problems of the flute embouchure (mouthpiece).

The *melodica*, a mouth organ fitted with push keys and a beak-shaped mouthpiece, is also very suitable for a young child to begin with. Also suitable for the younger child are small electronic instruments such as the *stylophone* and the *omnichord, chime bars*, the *autoharp* (or *chromaharp*), and the small *twelve-button accordion*.

———— Electronic instruments ————

During the past few years there have been many developments in the field of electronic music, and there is a wide choice of electronic keyboards, pianos, organs, synthesisers, computers and recording instruments. It is probable that some of these new developments may soon become outdated* and it is important, when contemplating a purchase, to study specifications of the different instruments and devices available (Yamaha, Roland, Technics, etc.).

Electronic keyboards vary in size from very small (suitable for children) to full size, with a large variety of sounds (e.g. piano, organ, harpsichord, saxophone, guitar), as well as drum and rhythm effects. Some keyboards have 'arrangers' which provide an accompaniment to whatever chords are played, in many different basic styles; also a 'composer' function which enables a performance to be recorded on the keyboard's memory, and another function which allows the player to transpose music into different keys. Some keyboards are part-organ, part-computer, and use a library of 'playcard' tunes which can be played back immediately.

* Laser technology, for example, is developing rapidly and it is possible that the compact disc, which has largely replaced the long-playing record, may itself be overtaken by the laser cassette, and the videocassette by the laservision disc.

Some of the more expensive electric (digital) pianos have a recognisable piano tone (though not as yet an *exact* imitation) and full-size weighted keys which are touch-sensitive (i.e. capable of being played with different degrees of loudness or softness). The compass is that of a normal piano and there are sustaining and soft pedals, and sometimes a third *sostenuto* pedal which allows the first note only to be sustained after the pedal is depressed. Most have facilities for cutting out the speakers, and listening through headphones when practising.

Such electric pianos are now accepted by examination boards as suitable for piano examinations.

Synthesisers

Music synthesisers consist of a group of electronic devices which can generate, modify and combine live sounds, imitate sounds of existing instruments, and create entirely new sounds. Pitches and other characteristics of sounds can be controlled by keyboards (often similar to black and white piano keyboards), and by panels of knobs and sliders. There is often a built-in 'sequencer', by which a series of pre-set rhythms can be controlled automatically. A digital sequencer may be used with some electric pianos (such as the Roland MT100) to play quick (floppy) discs of piano music (see page 67).

Relative cost of musical instruments

It is not possible to give exact estimates, but some general indication of the relative cost of different instruments may be of help. The relative cost relates to a new instrument suitable for a beginner, but secondhand instruments may be available at a lower cost, and hired ones at still less. The cost of better quality instruments will be considerably higher (e.g. a violin outfit for a beginner should cost only a moderate sum, whereas the cost of a violin suitable for a professional soloist would be very high indeed).

There are rental schemes which allow a piano or other instrument to be hired for three or six months, after which there is the option to return the instrument or to purchase it, when the hire charge would be deducted from the full price. Details may be obtained from most music shops.

Before buying or renting a wind instrument for a child, it may be as well to ask whether the school is prepared to lend one for a period, so that the child can discover whether he or she has a liking for the instrument, and is prepared to devote the necessary time to its study.

Low cost
Chime bars
Harmonica
Melodica
Recorder
Small electronic instruments
Small percussion instruments
(triangle, tambourine, etc.)
Tin whistle

Moderate cost
Accordion (small)
Banjo
Cello
Chromaharp (small)
Clarinet
Cornet
Flute
Guitar
Larger percussion instruments
(side drum, bass drum, etc.)
Mandolin
Small keyboard instruments
Trumpet
Trombone

Violin
Viola

Fairly high cost
Accordion (large)
Bassoon
Double bass
Electric piano
Euphonium
French horn
Large keyboard instruments
Oboe
Saxophone
Synthesiser
Tuba
Upright piano

Very high cost
Double bassoon
Electronic organ (large)
Grand piano
Harp
Harpsichord, etc.
Set of machine timpani
Xylophone, etc.

──── Practice and the neighbours ────

In considering the possibility of neighbours and those in your house objecting to your practice, especially in small flats, it should be borne in mind that some instruments (e. g. recorder) are much less obtrusive than others (e. g. trombone); also that some small pianos have a central pedal which reduces the volume of sound, and that the sound of some electric pianos and keyboards may be heard by the player through headphones.

─── **Summer music schools** ───

These offer music-making of all kinds, in a holiday atmosphere, and a good opportunity for practice. Details are published in the popular music journals (e. g. *Classical Music*).

The instruments described in this chapter and the singing voice will be dealt with in more detail in Chapters 4–7, but first the theory of music will be considered.

2

THE ABC OF MUSIC

———— The sound of music ————

Let us start with some definitions. The sensations of sound are caused by the vibrations of some object which, in turn, cause vibrations of the ear drum. If these vibrations are regular (e.g. vibrations of a piano or violin string) they are heard as musical sound; if irregular, as noise.

Musical sound has three characteristics:

1   **Pitch** (height or depth);
2   **Volume** (loudness or softness);
3   **Quality or tone-colour** (the effect upon the ear).

The pitch of sound is determined by the number of vibrations which produce it; the vibrations of a higher sound are more rapid than those of a lower sound. The lowest sound of a piano is played by the key on the extreme left of the keyboard on the longest string and, as the keys are played in order up the keyboard, the sounds become progressively higher (and the strings shorter), until the highest sound is reached by playing the key at the extreme right of the keyboard.

The power of a sound depends upon the width of the vibrations of the sounding body. A violin string, for example, may be made to vibrate over a wide or narrow space, and the wider the space the louder the sound will be. On the piano, a softer sound is obtained when a key is depressed slowly than when it is depressed quickly.

Sounds made by a piano, violin, flute or trumpet will produce different effects, even if the pitch and power are constant. This characteristic quality is called *timbre*, or tone-colour, and when music is scored for an orchestra, full use is made of the tone-colours of the different instruments. When simple sounds are arranged in succession, they form a *melody*. When three or more sounds of different pitch are heard together, they form a *chord*. Several chords in succession produce *harmony*.

Another factor in the sound of music is *rhythm*. Though not easy to define, rhythm is as essential to music as it is to poetry or prose. Rhythm takes in everything connected with the 'time' side of music (i.e. the distribution and accentuation of notes), but it goes deeper than this and implies a natural, 'breathing' performance, as opposed to mere mechanical time-keeping and accuracy. A melody without rhythm would lose its vitality, but rhythm can exist without melody (e.g. the beating of a drum).

Musical notation

Musical sounds may be represented by little oval characters called *notes*, which are named after the first seven letters of the alphabet, *A, B, C, D, E, F, G*.

The pitch of musical sounds may be shown by placing notes upon a set of parallel lines called a *stave*. Originally, the stave consisted of eleven lines (called the *Great Stave*) and notes were placed on these lines, and in the spaces between them.

Example 1

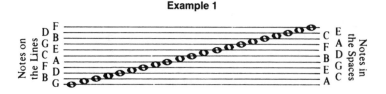

In more modern times the great stave was divided into two smaller staves, each of five lines, and the middle line was abolished, in order to make the notes easier to read. The two staves are distinguished from one another by the use of signs called *clefs*, which are placed at the beginning of the stave. The two clefs used in piano music are called the *treble clef* (&) and the *bass clef* (&). The two staves are joined together by a *brace*. In piano music the treble clef is normally used for the upper stave (played by the right hand), and the bass clef for the lower stave (played by the left hand); but sometimes, for convenience when playing high or low notes, the clefs are temporarily interchanged.

Example 2

In addition to the notes which can be placed on the lines and in the spaces of the treble and bass staves, one note can be placed above each stave, and another below.

Example 3

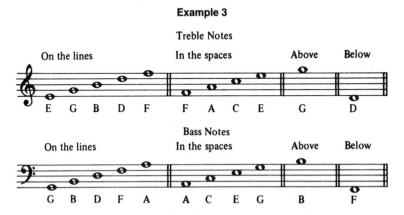

When the note on the middle (6th) line of the great stave is needed it is introduced on a short line either immediately below the treble stave or immediately above the bass stave.

Example 4

This note is called *Middle C* because it is the C nearest to the middle of the piano keyboard.

Leger lines

When sounds above or below the compass of either stave are needed, short lines called *leger lines* are added to the stave (the small line on which Middle C is written is, in fact, a leger line).

Example 5

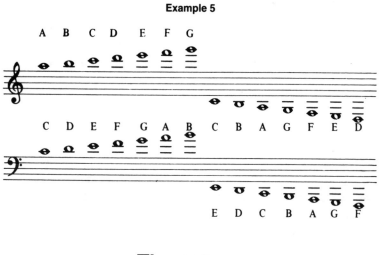

The octave

Since only seven different letter names are used in musical notation, these must be repeated when the series of notes is continued:

A,B,C,D,E,F,G   A,B,C,D,E,F,G   A,B,C,D,E,F,G . . .

Thus the eighth note of the series has the same letter name as the first, and is said to be an *octave* (eight notes) above it. Similarly, the first note is an octave below the eighth.

The sign *8ve* above a note means that the note is to be played an octave higher.

The sign *8ve* or *8ve bassa* below a note means that the note is to be played an octave lower. These signs avoid the use of many leger lines for very high or low notes, which are often difficult to read.

The sign *8* or *Con 8ve* below a note means that the written note and the note an octave below it are to be played together.

Note values

Different kinds of notes are used to show the length of a sound in relation to any other sound. The shape of the actual notehead is the same, but the centre can be left white, or blacked in, and different tails can be added. Example 6 shows the shape of each kind of note, and its relative value. Although English names are used in this book, it is also useful to know the American names, since they show at a glance the relative values, by dividing whole notes into fractions.*

Example 6

English Names   American Names

A Semibreve   Whole Note

is equal to 2 minims   Half Notes

or 4 Crotchets   Quarter Notes

* In $\frac{4}{2}$ time a note which lasts a whole bar is called a *breve*, and is written

or It is mainly found in old music.

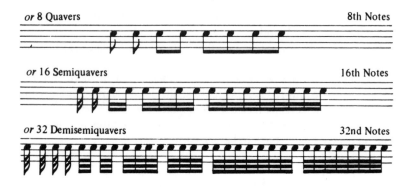

or 8 Quavers   8th Notes

or 16 Semiquavers   16th Notes

or 32 Demisemiquavers   32nd Notes

Dotted notes

A dot placed after a note increases its value by one half; two dots (less usual) increase its value by three-quarters.

Example 7

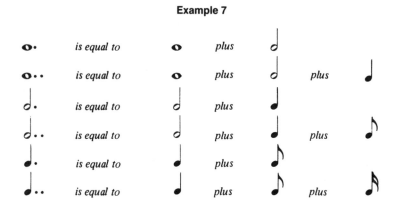

——— Tones and semitones ———

The difference in pitch between two sounds is called an *interval*. On the piano some adjacent white keys have a black key between them, and some do not. Adjacent white keys not separated by a black key are said to be a *semitone* (half-tone) apart, and those with a black key between them a *tone** (whole-tone) apart. Similarly, a black key is a semitone from the white key immediately above or below it.

Sharps, flats and naturals

The white keys of the piano form a series of natural notes, in other words notes which are neither sharp nor flat, which are named after the first seven letters of the alphabet. The black keys take their names from the white keys immediately above or below them, with the addition of *sharps* or *flats*. In musical notation, a sharp (♯) before a natural note raises the pitch by a semitone; a flat (♭) lowers the pitch by a semitone. Thus a sharp before C natural makes it C sharp, and a flat before D natural makes it D flat.

Example 8

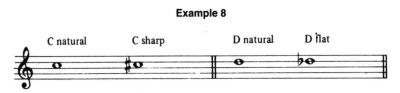

Since there is no black key between the white keys B and C, and E and F (i.e. they are a semitone apart), one white key does double duty for two notes with different names but the same sound. Example 9 shows a section of the piano keyboard. All the black keys, and four of the white keys, have alternative names. When two notes have the same sound (e.g. C sharp and D flat) but different names, they are called *enharmonics*.

---

* There is a distinction between British and American usage of the words 'tone' and 'note'. In British usage 'tone' usually means either (a) the interval of a major second (i.e. two semitones), or (b) the quality of a musical sound; and 'note' either (a) the actual written or printed sign which represents the pitch and duration of a musical sound, or (b) an actual sound of musical pitch; or (c) the finger-key of a piano, organ, etc. In American usage 'tone' (from the German *ton*) may be used to describe an actual sound of musical pitch, whereas 'note' is usually reserved for the written or printed sign. Thus 'three notes higher' (British) becomes 'three tones higher' (American).

Example 9

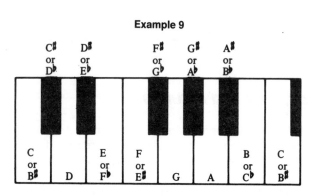

When a sharp or flat has been placed before a natural note, the original pitch can be restored to a subsequent note of the same letter name by placing a *natural* (♮) before it. In America this symbol is known as a *cancel*.

Example 10

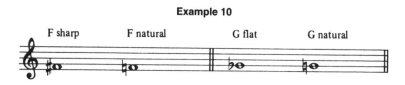

When one or more sharps or flats are placed immediately after a clef, they affect every note in the piece of music of the same letter-name, and are called *key-signatures* (see page 37). For example, an F sharp in the key-signature means that every F, no matter at what pitch it occurs, must be played as F sharp, unless a natural is placed before a particular F to indicate otherwise. Sharps or flats in a key-signature are known as *essentials*; their use makes music easier to read, since without them it would be necessary to insert sharps or flats each time they occur.

When a sharp or flat occurs during the *course* of a movement it is called an *accidental*, and affects only the note before which it is placed, and any notes of the same pitch which are included in the same bar (see next section).

Beats and bars

In music, as in poetry, there is a regular occurrence of strong and weak accents, or *beats*. Strong beats can be followed by one or more weaker beats, and beats can be grouped into rhythmic units called *measures*, or *bars*; the strong beats are shown by drawing vertical *bar-lines* across the stave. The British have come to use 'bar' for the interval of time between two bar-lines. The Americans more properly use 'measure', reserving 'bar' for (British) 'bar-line'.

Example 11

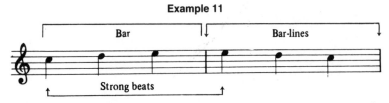

Each bar may consist of a group of two, three or four beats; normally the beat immediately after each bar-line is most strongly accented.*

Example 12

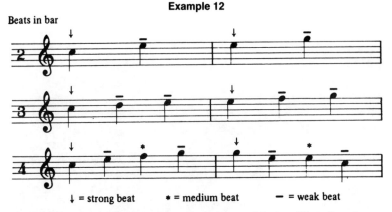

↓ = strong beat   * = medium beat   — = weak beat

* Melodies do not always start on the first beat of the bar. When they do not, the beat (or beats) preceding the first beat is known as an *anacrusis*. The beat (or beats) of the anacrusis is deducted from the beats of the final bar of the movement; thus, Handel's *Passepied* begins:

Fig. 2
Leonard Bernstein (1918–90), conductor of the New York Philharmonic Orchestra and a prolific composer of symphonies and musicals such as *West Side Story*.

Whereas bars of two or three beats consist of one strong beat followed by one (or two) weaker beats, the accents in a bar of four beats are strong on the first beat, medium on the third and weaker on the second and fourth.

Double bars, repeat marks and signs

Two vertical lines placed together are called a *double bar* (short for double bar-line), and are used at the end of a piece, or section of music. Two dots placed to the left of a double bar (called *repeat marks*) mean that the preceding section is to be repeated; placed to the right of a double bar, they mean that the section which follows is to be repeated.

Example 13

The words *1ma Volta* and *2da Volta* (1st and 2nd time), or the figures *1* and *2*, over a bar or bars of a repeated section, mean that the bar or bars marked *2da Volta* are to be played instead of the bar or bars marked *1ma Volta*, when the section is played a second time.

The sign *DC* (*Da Capo*) means 'Repeat from the beginning'; the sign *D𝄋* (*Dal Segno*) means 'Repeat from the sign 𝄋 '.

The word *Fine* (the end) is often placed over a double bar to show where a piece is to end, after the sign *DC* or *D𝄋* has been observed.

———— Time-signatures ————

The structure of the bars chosen by a composer for a particular section of music is shown by figures placed on the stave, immediately after the key-signature. These figures are called a *time-signature*, and they may also appear during the course of a movement if the original time-signature is changed.

Example 14

In simple time the upper figure shows the number of beats in each bar, the lower figure shows the value of each beat. Thus in Example 14 there are four beats to the bar, each of the value of one crotchet (quarter note).

The notes which make up a bar of music will not necessarily be of the same duration as the beats. In Example 15 bar one contains eight quavers, bar two contains two minims, bar three one minim, one crotchet and two quavers, and bar four one semibreve, but each bar contains the equivalent of four crotchets.

Example 15

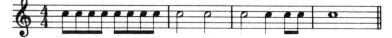

Similarly, a bar of $\frac{2}{4}$ contains two crotchets or the equivalent, and a bar of $\frac{3}{4}$ three crotchets or the equivalent.

When each beat of a bar can be divided into halves, quarters, etc., this is called *simple time*. Alternatively, when each beat has the value of a dotted note, and is divisible into thirds, sixths, etc., this is called *compound time*. In compound times the lower figure of the time-signature shows the *divisions* of the beats; thus in $\frac{6}{8}$ time the total value of the bar is equal to six quavers, but the actual beats are dotted crotchets.

Example 16

Example 17 shows the time-signatures in common use, together with the value in notes of one complete bar. Bars which may be divided into two, three or four equal beats are said to be, respectively, in duple, triple and quadruple time. $\frac{4}{4}$ time is sometimes referred to as *common time* and given the sign c ; $\frac{2}{2}$ time is sometimes called *Alla Breve* and given the sign ¢ ; these signs are more often found in older music.

Example 17

TABLE OF TIME-SIGNATURES

	SIMPLE TIMES		COMPOUND TIMES	
	Time-Signature	Value of one bar	Time-Signature	Value of one bar
DUPLE	¢ or $\frac{2}{2}$ $\frac{2}{4}$ $\frac{2}{8}$	𝅝 𝅝 ♩ ♩ ♪ ♪	$\frac{6}{4}$ $\frac{6}{8}$ $\frac{6}{16}$	𝅗𝅥. 𝅗𝅥. ♩. ♩. ♪. ♪.
TRIPLE	$\frac{3}{2}$ $\frac{3}{4}$ $\frac{3}{8}$	𝅝 𝅝 𝅝 ♩ ♩ ♩ ♪ ♪ ♪	$\frac{9}{4}$ $\frac{9}{8}$ $\frac{9}{16}$	𝅗𝅥. 𝅗𝅥. 𝅗𝅥. ♩. ♩. ♩. ♪. ♪. ♪.
QUADRUPLE	$\frac{4}{2}$ C or $\frac{4}{4}$ $\frac{4}{8}$	𝅝 𝅝 𝅝 𝅝 ♩ ♩ ♩ ♩ ♪ ♪ ♪ ♪	$\frac{12}{4}$ $\frac{12}{8}$ $\frac{12}{16}$	𝅗𝅥. 𝅗𝅥. 𝅗𝅥. 𝅗𝅥. ♩. ♩. ♩. ♩. ♪. ♪. ♪. ♪.

Composers also use mixed bars. Thus, a signature of $\frac{5}{4}$ may be regarded as $\frac{3}{4} + \frac{2}{4}$, or $\frac{2}{4} + \frac{3}{4}$ as in Example 18.

Example 18

Symphony No. 6 Tchaikovsky

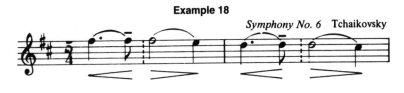

Similarly, a signature of $\frac{7}{4}$ may be regarded as $\frac{4}{4} + \frac{3}{4}$, or $\frac{3}{4} + \frac{4}{4}$. Bars with 11 or 13 beats may also be used.

The tie

A sound may be prolonged by joining two or more notes of *the same pitch* together with a short curved line, called a *tie*. The effect is that the first note is sustained for its own length and the length of the tied notes, which are not sounded.

Example 19

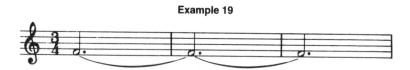

The tie must not be confused with the *slur,* which is a curved line placed over or under a group of two or more notes of *different pitch* to indicate phrasing (see page 50) or, on a stringed instrument, to be played in one bow.

Grouping of notes

Notes are often grouped together by joining the hooks of their tails.

Example 20

In simple times notes may be grouped into twos, fours, eights, etc. In compound times they may be grouped into threes, sixes, etc.

Example 21

Sometimes three notes may be played in the time of two notes of similar value. The group of three notes is then called a *triplet*, and the sign placed above, or below, it.

Example 22

Other irregular groupings are sometimes used.

Name	Sign	Effect
Duplet	⌒2	Two notes played in the time of three.
Quadruplet	⌒4	Four notes played in the time of three.
Quintuplet	⌒5	Five notes played in the time of four.
Sextolet	⌒6	Six notes played in the time of four.
Septuplet	⌒7	Seven notes played in the time of four (or, occasionally, six)

—————————————— **Rests** ——————————————

In music there are often short periods of silence between sounds, which are represented by signs called *rests*, each equivalent to a note of the same value.* A bar may consist entirely of notes or rests, or partly of

* A breve rest (mostly found in old music) is written ▬▬ .

notes and partly of rests, so long as it is of the exact value indicated by the time-signature.

Example 23

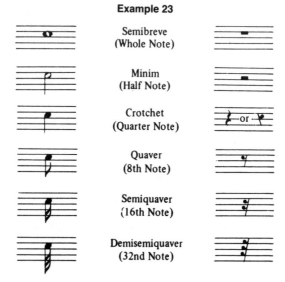

Semibreve (Whole Note)		
Minim (Half Note)		
Crotchet (Quarter Note)		
Quaver (8th Note)		
Semiquaver (16th Note)		
Demisemiquaver (32nd Note)		

Some rests are rather similar, and may be confused. The semibreve rest *hangs* from the fourth line of the stave, whereas the minim rest *sits* on the third line. When the sign ⌐ is used to represent the crotchet rest (mainly in hand-written music) the hook is to the right. The sign for the quaver rest is similar, but the hook is to the left.

A silent bar is indicated by a semibreve rest; several bars' silence is shown by a rest with a number over it.

Example 24

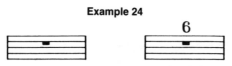

A pause sign ⌒ over a note or rest means that it is to be prolonged – the exact length is left to the performer's discretion.

Example 25

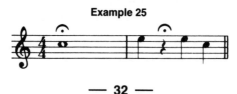

Dynamics

Words, abbreviations and signs which indicate degrees of loudness and softness of sounds are called *dynamics*; e.g. *piano* (p) = soft, *forte* (f) = loud, *crescendo* (*cres.* or <) = increasing in volume, *decrescendo* (*decres.* or >) = decreasing in volume (see Glossary of Musical Terms, page 218).

Scales

A scale may be thought of as a ladder of notes arranged in alphabetical order to form an octave. However, if we ascend or descend the notes of a scale one by one, the sounds will not all be the same distance apart, except for the chromatic scale which consists entirely of semitones (see page 34).

In medieval times church music was based on a system of seven different *modal* scales, which may be heard by playing a succession of seven white keys on the piano, starting on each note in turn. Two of these seven-note scales have survived in modern music – they are called *diatonic* scales (from the Greek 'through the tones') – and are of two kinds, *major* and *minor*. The major scale is based on the *Ionian Mode*, the minor scale on the *Aeolian Mode* (see page 37).

Degrees of the scale

Each note of the diatonic scale is called a *degree* and is given a name, though it is often more convenient to use Roman numerals, as in Example 26.

Example 26

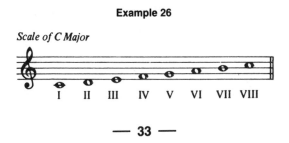

Scale of C Major

I   II   III   IV   V   VI   VII   VIII

The names of the degrees, which are counted upwards, are shown below. In Tonic Sol-fa a similar system of naming degrees is used.

Degree	Name	Tonic Sol-fa Name
I	*tonic,* or *key-note*	DOH
II	*supertonic*	RAY
III	*mediant*	ME
IV	*subdominant*	FAH
V	*dominant*	SO
VI	*submediant*[1]	LAH
VII	*leading note*[2]	TE
VIII	*tonic,* or *key-note*	DOH

[1] This is sometimes the American 'superdominant'.
[2] Sometimes this becomes the American 'subtonic' or 'leading tone'.

The eighth degree is, of course, a repetition of the tonic or key-note, an octave higher in pitch. The dominant, as its name implies, is the 'ruling' note of the scale. Next in importance is the tonic, which is the 'governing' note. Third in importance is the fourth degree, the subdominant. Chords formed on these three notes may be used to form three kinds of 'cadences' (see page 145). The seventh degree is called the leading note because of its strong tendency to lead to the tonic.

Intervals

An interval is the difference in pitch between two notes. It is calculated by counting the letter names upwards, from the lower to the higher note. Thus, C to D is a second, C to E a third, and so on.

Semitones (the smallest intervals in modern music) can be of two kinds:

1 Semitones formed by two notes having different letter names (e.g. B to C, F sharp to G) are called *diatonic* because they occur in major or minor (diatonic) scales.
2 Semitones formed by two notes having the same letter name (e.g. C to C sharp, D to D sharp) are called *chromatic* because they occur only in chromatic scales.

Intervals may be *perfect, major, minor, diminished* or *augmented.* Any interval which is counted from the first note of a major scale to any other note of that scale must be either major or perfect. *

Example 27

A major interval, if decreased by a semitone (by flattening the upper note or sharpening the lower note), becomes minor. Thus C to E flat, and C sharp to E natural are minor thirds. A perfect or major interval, if increased by a semitone, becomes augmented (e.g. C to D sharp, and C flat to D natural are augmented seconds). A perfect or minor interval, if decreased by a semitone, becomes diminished (e.g. C to G flat, and C sharp to G natural are diminished fifths).

Note that two intervals which have identical pitch, but different letter names, will be differently described. Thus, C to E flat is a minor third, but C to D sharp is an augmented second.

Example 28

An interval may be *inverted* by placing either the top note an octave lower, or the bottom note an octave higher. Perfect intervals, when inverted, remain perfect; minor intervals become major; major intervals become minor; augmented intervals become diminished, and diminished intervals augmented.

* The unison, formed by two notes of the same pitch and letter name, and shown thus

is often called perfect, though strictly speaking it is not an interval at all.

An interval which does not exceed the compass of an octave is said to be *simple*; one which does exceed it is said to be *compound*. A compound interval is a simple interval to which an octave is added, and may be reduced to a simple interval by subtracting seven. Thus a ninth (9−7=2) becomes a second, a tenth (10−7=3) a third, and so on.

Example 29

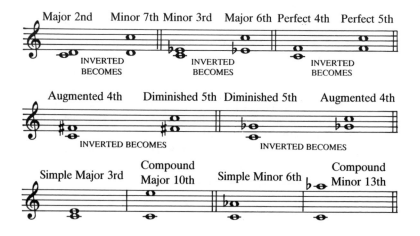

Intervals which appeal to the ear as complete in themselves, and do not require another sound to follow are said to be *consonant*. Intervals which leave a sense of incompleteness, and a desire for resolution into some other sound, are said to be *dissonant*. Perfect intervals, and major and minor thirds and sixths, are usually classed as consonant; major and minor seconds and sevenths, and augmented and diminished intervals, as dissonant. For instance, the first interval in Example 30 (a dissonant augmented fourth) sounds incomplete until it is resolved into the second interval (a consonant minor sixth).

Example 30

There is, however, no wholly satisfactory definition of consonant and dissonant intervals, and in twentieth-century music the distinction has become largely obsolete.

Chords

A *chord* normally consists of three or more notes which are sounded together. A two-note chord is possible if a third note is *implied,* though it is more often called an interval.

Example 31

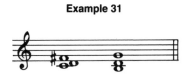

The pattern of major scales, and key-signatures

The major scale is made up of tones and semitones arranged according to a definite plan – there is an interval of a semitone between the third and fourth, and seventh and eighth degrees, and a tone between any other two adjacent notes. The major scale may thus be divided into two halves, each with the same pattern (tone-tone-semitone). Each half is called a *tetrachord* (a Greek word applied to the four strings of an early instrument), and the two tetrachords are joined by an interval of a tone.

Example 32

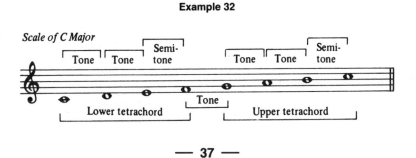

A piece of music which is founded on the C major scale is said to be in the *key* of C major.

Every major scale is constructed according to the same pattern. If we take the *upper* tetrachord of the scale of C major, and add a tetrachord above it, we form the scale of G major.

Example 33

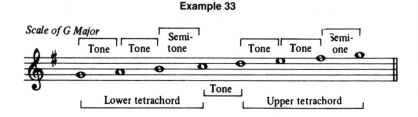

The first degree (i.e. the tonic, or key-note) of the new scale is G (i.e. the fifth degree, or dominant, of C major). To make the upper tetrachord of the new scale conform to the regular pattern – tone, tone, semitone – the third note must be raised a semitone. Thus, in the scale of G major the seventh degree (F) is sharpened. This sharp, which is vital to the construction of the new scale, is therefore used as a *key-signature* (see page 24).

By taking the *upper* tetrachord of the scale of G major, and adding a tetrachord *above* it, we may form the scale of D major. Again the dominant of G major becomes the tonic of D major, and the seventh degree of the scale must be raised a semitone, by adding another sharp to the key-signature.

Example 34

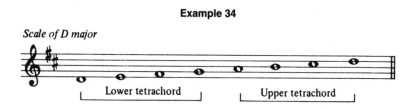

By continuing the process we may form, successively, the major scales of A, E, B, F sharp, and C sharp (seldom used by composers). Each time, the dominant of the old scale becomes the tonic of the new one, and the seventh degree of the new scale is raised a semitone by adding a further sharp to the key-signature.

Example 35

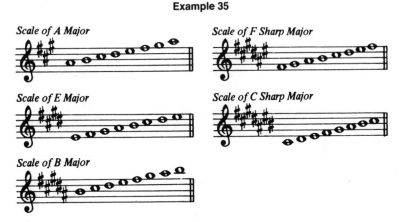

Scale of A Major

Scale of F Sharp Major

Scale of E Major

Scale of C Sharp Major

Scale of B Major

If we take the *lower* tetrachord of the scale of C major, and add a tetrachord *below* it, we may form the scale of F major, the first of the series of major scales with one or more flats in the key-signature.

Example 36

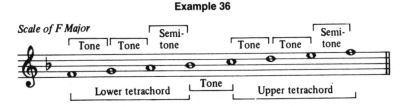

Scale of F Major

Tone | Tone | Semi-tone | Tone | Tone | Semi-tone

Lower tetrachord | Tone | Upper tetrachord

Notice firstly that the tonic of the old scale becomes the dominant of the new one; and secondly that to obtain a semitone between the third and fourth degrees, and a tone between the two tetrachords, the fourth degree of the new scale must be lowered a semitone, by giving the scale a key-signature of one flat.

Continuing with the process we may form, successively, the major scales of B flat, E flat, A flat, D flat, G flat and C flat. Each time, the fourth degree of the new scale is lowered by adding another flat to the key-signature.

Example 37

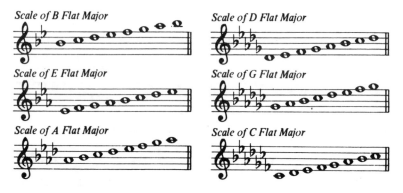

Scale of B Flat Major

Scale of D Flat Major

Scale of E Flat Major

Scale of G Flat Major

Scale of A Flat Major

Scale of C Flat Major

The minor scale

The second kind of diatonic scale – the minor scale – is often chosen when a composer wishes to write sad or expressive music (e.g. Beethoven's *Sonata Pathétique* (1799)), though there is, of course, much expressive music in major keys.*

During the past few centuries the major scale has remained unaltered, while the minor scale has undergone several changes. The earliest form is based on the modal scale starting on A, illustrated in Example 38.

Example 38

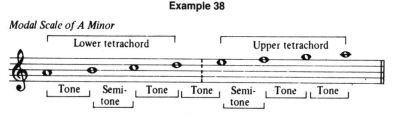

Modal Scale of A Minor

Lower tetrachord — Upper tetrachord

Tone | Semi-tone | Tone | Tone | Semi-tone | Tone | Tone

Although, like the scale of C major, the above scale is formed of natural notes (played on the white piano keys), the pattern of the lower and

---

* The sad effect is largely due to the flattened third scale, which gives the minor scale its character. If the harmonic minor scale of A (Ex. 39) is compared with the scale of A major (Ex. 35), it will be seen that both the third and the sixth notes of the minor scale are flattened (i.e. are a semitone lower than in the major scale).

upper tetrachords is not the same – lower tetrachord tone-semitone-tone, upper tetrachord semitone-tone-tone.

In order to produce a semitone between the seventh and eighth degrees (one of the characteristics of our modern scale system), the modal scale is usually modified in modern use. One way of doing this is to sharpen the seventh note, thus forming what is known as the *harmonic minor* scale. Again the pattern of the two tetrachords is different.

Example 39

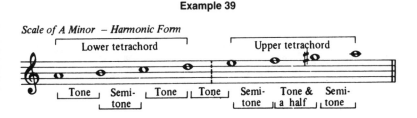

Scale of A Minor – Harmonic Form

Although the seventh note of this scale is sharpened, the sharp is not included in the key-signature, but is regarded as an accidental. However, by sharpening the seventh degree of the scale the interval between the sixth and seventh degrees becomes an augmented second (tone-and-a-half). This interval was considered difficult to sing, and to overcome this objection the *melodic minor scale* was evolved. This scale, as its name implies, was originally used chiefly for the construction of melodies, whereas the harmonic minor scale was used chiefly in the construction of chords (harmony).

A peculiarity of the melodic minor scale is that different forms are used when ascending and descending. In ascending, the sixth and seventh notes are sharpened; in descending they are restored to their original pitch. The descending form is therefore that of the modal minor scale. Again these sharpened notes are not included in the key-signature, but are regarded as accidentals (Example 40).

Major and minor scales which have the same key-signature (e.g. C major and A minor) are said to be *relative* to one another. Each major scale has its *relative minor*, the first note of the minor scale being the sixth note of the relative major. Looking at it another way, the last three notes of the major scale become the first three notes of the relative minor.

A minor scale which starts on the same note (tonic) as a major scale is

Example 40

Scale of A Minor – Melodic Form

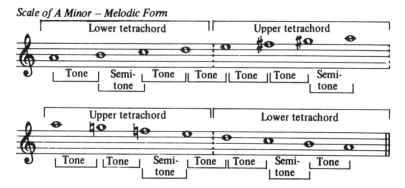

known as its *tonic minor*, but a glance at Example 41 will show that the key-signature of a major scale and its tonic minor are not the same; D major, for example, has a key-signature of two sharps, and D minor of one flat.

Example 41

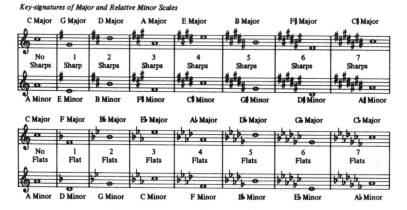

To form the 'sharp' series of minor scales we take the *upper* tetrachord of a scale and add a tetrachord *above* it. Thus, the modal scale of E minor is formed by taking the upper tetrachord of the modal scale of A minor and adding above it a tetrachord consisting of semitone-tone-semitone. Since E minor is relative to G major, it will have a key-signature of one sharp.

Example 42

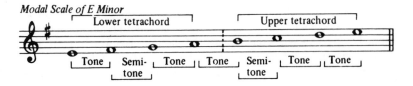

Modal Scale of E Minor

We may now turn the modal scale into the harmonic and melodic forms.

To form the harmonic scale (Example 43) we sharpen the seventh note with an accidental.

Example 43

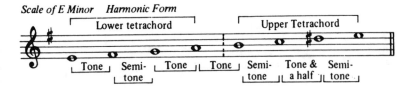

Scale of E Minor   Harmonic Form

To form the melodic scale (Example 44), when ascending we sharpen the sixth and seventh notes; when descending we restore these notes to their original pitch.

Continuing the process we may form the other minor scales which

Example 44

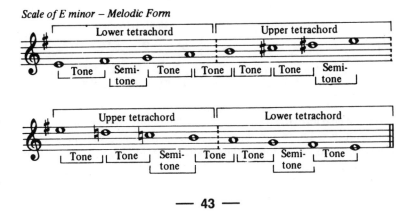

Scale of E minor – Melodic Form

have sharps in their key-signatures: B minor, F sharp minor, C sharp minor, G sharp minor, D sharp minor and A sharp minor (seldom used).

The 'flat' series of minor scales is formed by taking the *lower* tetra-chord of a modal minor scale, and adding a tetrachord *below* it. The tonic of one key thus becomes the dominant of another. To form the pattern of the new upper tetrachord we must modify the pattern of the old (lower) tetrachord. Thus when taking the lower tetrachord of the modal A minor scale, and adding a tetrachord below it to form the modal D minor scale, we add a key-signature of one flat, to produce a semitone between the fifth and sixth degrees of the scale.

Example 45

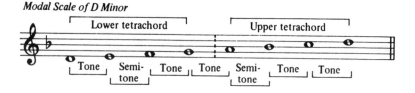

From the modal scale of D minor, we can form the harmonic scale of D minor, by sharpening the seventh note with an accidental.

Example 46

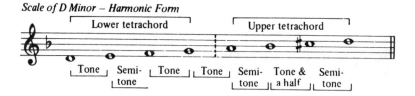

We can also form the melodic scale of D minor by sharpening the sixth and seventh notes of the modal scale by means of accidentals when ascending, and by restoring these notes to their original pitch when descending.

Example 47

Scale of D Minor – Melodic Form

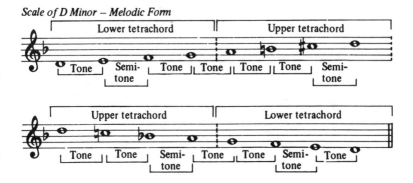

By the same process we can form the other minor scales which have flats in their key-signature: G minor, C minor, F minor, B flat minor, E flat minor and A flat minor (seldom used).

The Circle of Fifths

The relationship of the major and relative minor keys may be demonstrated by the Circle of Fifths (see Example 48 overleaf), in which the keys are arranged in order of ascending and descending fifths, starting with C major (A minor).

The order of sharp keys goes up in fifths (clockwise from C major), the dominant of one key becoming the tonic of the next.

The order of flat keys goes down in fifths (anti-clockwise from C major), the tonic of one key becoming the dominant of the next.

The chromatic scale

The *chromatic scale* consists entirely of semitones, and each octave contains twelve different notes arranged in alphabetical order, though there may be two notes of the same letter name: C and C sharp, D and D flat, and so on. On the piano all the keys, white and black, are used in order. The chromatic scale is usually formed by taking the notes of the major scale and filling in the missing semitones, sharpening the notes in

Example 48

The Circle of Fifths

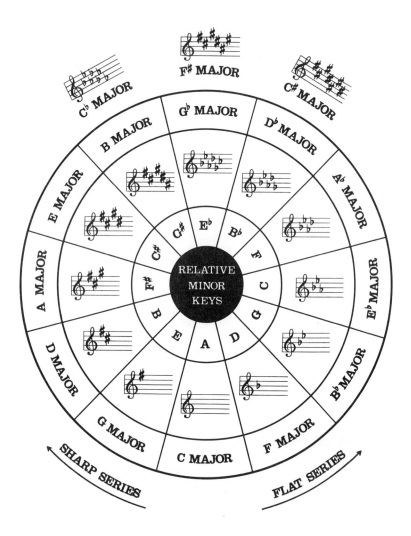

ascending, and flattening them in descending. Example 49 shows the chromatic scale starting on C – the white-headed notes are those of the major scale, and the black-headed notes those added to form the chromatic scale.

Example 49

Another method of writing this scale is sometimes asked for in examination questions; it is called the *harmonic chromatic scale*, in which the tonic and dominant letter names are used only once.

Example 50

The pentatonic scale

This is one of the oldest known scales, which is used in Scottish and Irish folk music (e.g. *Auld Lang Syne*) as well as in traditional music of Central Europe and the Far East, and in Negro music (e.g. *Deep River*). It has also been used by modern composers such as Debussy and Ravel.

It is called a *gapped* scale, since it contains only five notes to the octave, e.g. C,D,F,G,A, and may therefore be played on the black keys of the piano.

Example 51

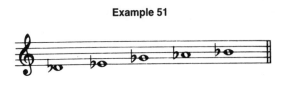

The whole-tone scale

This scale, consisting of whole-tones only, has been used by Debussy, Liszt, Glinka and others. There is no implicit relationship between the notes of the scale (in the sense of the tonic and dominant of the diatonic scale).

Example 52

Another possible version is D flat, E flat, F,G,A,B,C sharp (or D flat).

── Double-sharps and double-flats ──

The pitch of a natural note may be raised by a tone by placing the sign 𝄪 (double-sharp) before it, or lowered by a tone by placing the sign ♭♭ (double-flat) before it. Double-sharps and double-flats occur only during the course of a movement, and are therefore accidentals. A note which has already been sharpened or flattened may be raised or lowered by a further semitone by means of a double-sharp or double-flat. A double-sharp or double-flat may be reduced to a single sharp or flat by the signs ♮♯ or ♮♭. Alternatively, the signs for a single sharp or flat may be used.

Example 53

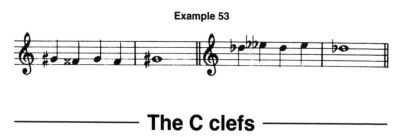

─────────── The C clefs ───────────

From the great stave it is possible to select the five highest lines to form the treble clef, and the five lowest lines to form the bass clef. These two clefs are said to be 'fixed', because they always occupy the same position on the stave. It is also possible to select five consecutive lines from the great stave other than those of the treble and bass clefs, which will more conveniently represent the sounds of voices and instruments of medium pitch. When this happens a clef called the *C clef* is used. This is said to be 'movable', because it may be placed in more than one position on the stave.

Example 54

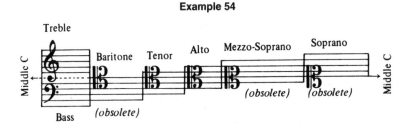

The C clef is placed on the stave in such a way that it indicates the position of Middle C. There are five kinds of C clefs, two of which, the *alto* and *tenor*, are in use today. The other three are obsolete, but may be found in old music. The signs for the C clefs, and the relation with the treble and bass clefs, are shown in Example 54.

In Example 55 a passage is written in the treble, bass, alto and tenor clefs. The effect in each case is precisely the same.

Example 55

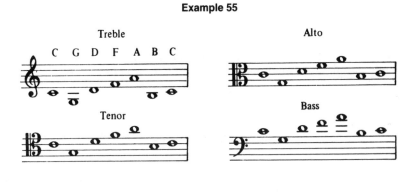

Syncopation

Syncopation is the displacement of a regular accent, so that it falls on that part of a bar not usually accented. Example 56 shows two different ways of effecting syncopation. In bars one and three an accented note is placed on an unaccented beat; the altered accent is marked with a *stress* sign (>). In bars two and four a note on an unaccented beat is tied to a note on an accented beat.

Example 56

Phrasing marks

A melody is divided into small units called *phrases*; these give the melody shape, and allow it to breathe. Four-bar phrases are common, but a phrase may consist of any number of bars. Various marks are used by composers to show how they wish their music to be phrased.

A *slur* (not to be confused with a tie – see page 30) is a curved line placed over or under two or more notes of different pitch. In instrumental music the slur means that the notes under or over it are to be played as smoothly as possible (i.e. *legato*: It. 'smooth'). In vocal music the slur is often used when two or more notes are to be sung to one syllable.

Example 57

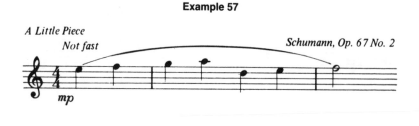

In contrast to *legato*, music may also be performed in a crisp style known as *staccato* (It. 'detached'). *Staccato* notes are indicated by dots placed over or under them, and are usually given approximately half their written value, though this depends on the speed and style of the music. Notes to be played even shorter (*staccatissimo*) may be marked with a pointed dash (˅) – which earlier composers such as Haydn and Beethoven sometimes used to indicate a less rigid *staccato* – and notes to be only slightly detached (*mezzo-staccato*) with a combination of a dot and a slur, or a dot and a short line.

Example 58

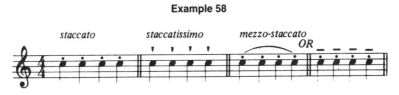

Accents

The *accent* sign >, placed over or under a note, means that the note is to be stressed; the sign ∧ indicates an even stronger accent. The sign — (sometimes called *tenuto* (> It. 'to hold') means that the note so marked is to be held for its full length, and usually also slightly stressed; this sign is often used after a *staccato* note.

Arpeggios, broken chords and glissando

Arpeggios (It. 'harplike') are chords, the notes of which instead of being sounded together are played one after the other. The notes of a chord may also be played in rapid succession, usually from the bottom upwards, when they are said to be *spread* (indicated by a curved or wavy line).

Broken chords are similar to *arpeggios*, except that the notes are not played in consecutive order.

Glissando (It. from the Fr. *glisser* 'to glide') is the rapid sliding of the finger over the keys of the piano, the strings of the harp, or between notes on the same string of a violin, etc. It is usually indicated by a straight or wavy oblique line between notes, and/or the word *gliss.*

Example 59

Ornaments

Ornaments are decorations or embellishments of the notes of a melody, without altering the basic pulse of the music. Up to the 18th century, performers usually improvised their embellishments, but later composers often indicated ornaments by small notes (called 'grace notes') or signs, which were placed before, after, or over the principal note. The more usual ornaments are:

The **appoggiatura** (It. 'to lean'), a small note written before the principal note, and taking half its value if it is undotted, and two-thirds if it is dotted.

Example 60

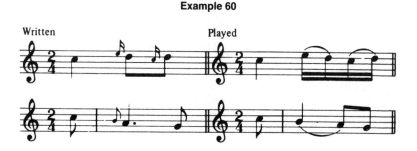

Modern composers usually give the *appoggiatura* its proper written value.

The **acciaccatura** (It. 'crushing'), written like the *appoggiatura*, but with a slanting stroke through the stem. It is sounded on (or just before) the beat, as quickly as possible before the principal note. Pianists sometimes play the *acciaccatura* and the principal note together, releasing the *acciaccatura* and holding the principal note.

Example 61

The **turn** (sign ∾ placed over or after a note), a figure of four notes (note above, note itself, note below, note itself). This figure is played either instead of, or after, the note itself.

Example 62

A sharp or flat, placed above or below the turn, means that the upper or lower note is to be sharpened or flattened.

Example 63

The **inverted turn** (sign ↭ or ⌇) is played like the turn, except that the figure is the note below, note itself, note above and note itself.

The **upper mordent** (sign ᷈) consists of three notes (note itself, note above, and note itself) played in rapid succession.

Example 64

The **lower mordent** (sign ᷈) is played in the same way, except that the three notes consist of the note itself, note below, and note itself.

The **trill** or shake (sign 𝄐 ᷈) consists of the rapid alternation of the written note and the note above. The trill usually ends with a turn.

Example 65

In baroque, see page 179 (and sometimes later) music, it is usual to begin a trill on the note above the written note, which produces an even number of notes (this also applies to any period when the written note is preceded by a note of the same pitch). Romantic and modern composers usually include a preliminary grace note when they intend a trill to begin on a note other than the written note.

In well-edited editions of baroque and classical music, suggestions for the performance of ornaments are usually shown as footnotes. Further study of this complex subject may be pursued through such books as *Keyboard Interpretation* by Howard Ferguson (Oxford University Press).

How to write music

Good musical handwriting can be acquired by practice, and the careful study of printed music. Twelve-stave 'quarto' music paper measuring 30.4×24.15 cm (about $12'' \times 9\frac{1}{2}''$) is suitable for most purposes, though for orchestral and choral music larger paper, with more staves, may be needed. A black felt-tipped pen is usually a suitable writing implement.

Practise copying printed clefs, and notice that the central curve of the treble clef encloses the G line, and the two dots in the bass clef are on either side of the F line; these clefs are also known as G and F clefs. The two C clefs in common use may be written:

Example 66

Lay out notes and bars with care, so that they are well spaced and easy to read. Study the way this is done in printed music. Normally, when two or more quavers (semiquavers, etc.) are grouped together their tails are joined. As many notes are joined together as will represent one beat.

Example 67

Sonata in C major K 545, Mozart

There are several exceptions: if, for example, in a bar of $\frac{4}{4}$ time the first (or last) half of the bar consists of quavers, these are grouped together.

Example 68

Sonatina, Op. 36, No 1, Clementi

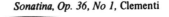

Similarly, the four quavers in a bar of $\frac{2}{4}$ are grouped together; also the six quavers in a bar of $\frac{3}{4}$, and the three quavers (or six semiquavers) in a bar of $\frac{3}{8}$.

Example 69

Sometimes, to indicate phrasing, the grouping is split.

Example 70

Here again careful study of printed music will reveal other exceptions to normal grouping, which are too numerous to list.

To make handwritten music easy to read, and to achieve good results in examinations, take special care that sharps and flats are in the correct order and position on the stave. When writing quavers, semiquavers, etc., as a general rule the stems of single notes above the middle line should point downwards to the left, and these of notes below the middle line, upwards to the right. Notes on the middle line may point either way, according to the context of the music. Similarly, when grouped notes have joined stems, with some notes above the middle line and others below it, the majority of notes (above or below) will generally decide the direction.

Example 71

So far as possible, leger lines should be written at the same distance from one another as are the lines of the stave, and should be reasonably consistent in length. Very high or low leger notes, which are difficult to read and may take up too much space, can usually be avoided by the use of *8va* signs. Finally, be careful to include exact details of phrasing, speed, dynamics, etc.

Transposition

Transposition is writing music at a higher or lower pitch than that in which it was originally written. There are many reasons for transposing music; for example, a soprano song may need to be put into another key if it is sung by a contralto or bass (see also 'Clefs and Transposing Instruments', page 137).

The simplest transposition is up or down to a different octave; the key (and the key-signature) will remain the same, though the clef may be changed.

Example 72

Original melody   Transposed up an octave

Transposed down an octave

Transposition to any other interval (e.g. up a perfect fifth, or down a minor third) means that the transposed version will be in a different key to the original, with a different key-signature. Example 73 shows a melody transposed (a) up a perfect fifth, and (b) down a minor third. The process of transposing is as follows:

1   Look at the key and key-signature of the original melody (regard this as a *major* key-signature, whether or not the melody is in a major or minor key). Regard the melody in Example 72, therefore, as in the key of E flat major, with a key-signature of three flats.

2   Decide on the *new* key-signature. A perfect fifth above E flat is B flat, so the transposed version will be in the key of B flat, with a key-signature of two flats. A minor third below E flat is C, so the transposed version will be in the key of C major, with no key-signature (i.e. no sharps or flats).

3   Next write the transposed version of the melody either five notes above or three below the original. Finally, every accidental in the original melody must be added to the transposed versions. Thus, the fourth and sixth notes of the original melody are each raised by a semitone (E natural and F sharp). In the transposed versions these notes must also be raised by a semitone (B natural and C sharp; or C sharp and D sharp). When adding accidentals, the key-signatures of the original melody and of the transposed version must always be taken into account.

Example 73

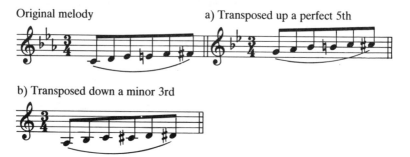

Repetition and reiteration of bars and notes

In written, and sometimes printed, music shorthand signs may be used when bars or notes are to be repeated.

Example 74

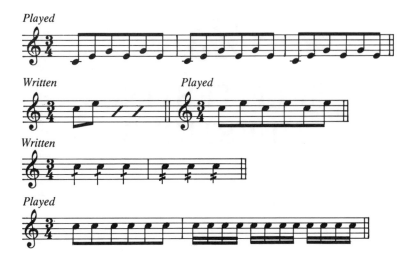

2a

SELF-TESTING QUESTIONS

1 Name the key, and add a suitable time-signature, bar-lines and phrasing.

2 Add rests to complete these bars:

3 Describe the intervals marked (a), (b), (c) and (d).

4 Write, in the bass clef with key-signature, one octave (ascending and descending) of the melodic scale of G minor.

5   Write out the ornaments in full.

Answers on page 239.

3

——— PRACTISING ———

The professional concert artist needs not only an exceptional degree of musical talent, but also the capacity to devote many hours daily to the practice and study of music. The amateur performer will probably have many other commitments, and practice will only be possible on a limited scale. But whether practice is for half-an-hour or six hours a day, the general principles are the same. Practice consists of repetition, but repetition is only valuable if there is reason and thought behind it, and aimless repetition may actually develop and perfect the faults which the performer is trying to eradicate.

In the early stages of studying a musical instrument, or singing, different parts of the body will be subjected to unfamiliar kinds of muscular exertion (or breathing, etc.). Practice periods should be quite short, with a few moments of mental or physical relaxation whenever concentration begins to flag or tension creeps in.

Practice is a very personal experience, and it is not possible to lay down rigid rules, but there are some general principles which will be found useful. Let us suppose you are about to practise music you have never seen before.

——— Before you start to play ———

Look through the music slowly and carefully, trying to hear it in your 'mind's ear'. Find out the key of the piece. The key-signature will give a clue, but a key-signature of one sharp, for example, means that the key is either G major or E minor (its relative). The lowest note of the first chord and of the last chord may give a clue (in piano music, etc.), and if the key is E minor the presence of the sharpened seventh (D sharp) would tend to confirm this. Note that the key and the key-signature may be changed during the course of a movement.

Look at the time-signature, and decide at what speed the piece should be played. The time-signature shows the number of beats in a bar (⁴₄ four crotchet beats, ⁶₈ two dotted crotchet beats, etc.), and the Italian term (or German, French, English, etc.) will give an approximate idea of the speed (*Adagio*, *Presto*, etc.). There may also be a metronome mark which will give a more precise indication. (The metronome is a clock-like instrument with a flat steel pendulum which swings from side to side with a click;* the speed can be adjusted by moving a weight up and down the pendulum. A graduated scale behind the pendulum covers a range from 40 to 208 ticks (beats) to the minute. Thus (♩ = 120) means that the metronome is to be set to give 120 ticks to the minute, each crotchet having the value of one tick.)

Note the phrasing, carefully distinguishing between *legato* (slurred) and *staccato* (with dots over or under the notes). Try to imagine the appropriate style. Some pieces have obvious clues – 'Menuet', 'Bourrée' or 'Waltz' mean that the pieces are to be performed in the style of these dances. The style of other pieces must be judged by phrasing, melody, harmony, texture, etc. This skill will be acquired gradually through experience.

——— When you start to play ———

Practise one thing at a time. When playing a new piece of piano music, for example, start with a small section (perhaps four bars), and practise each

---

* There are also small battery-powered metronomes.

hand separately, making sure that you are playing the right notes in the right time, and with the right fingering. Only when you can play each hand correctly can you expect to co-ordinate the hands.

Take special care when counting the time. In slow music it is often useful to sub-divide the beat – music in $\frac{2}{4}$ time could be counted 1 *and* 2 *and*, music in $\frac{6}{8}$ time as six quavers instead of two dotted crotchets, and so on. The metronome may sometimes be useful for checking possible deviations from the beat, while trying to play strictly in time.

When you have learnt to play the notes correctly and in time, you will be able to consider other aspects of the music (e. g. use of the pedals, if any, dynamics, interpretation, etc.). Difficult passages should be isolated, and worked at one at a time. Do not fall into the habit of always starting at the beginning of a piece; although it must be played right through on occasions, most time needs to be spent on the most difficult bars. It is important that you should be able to start on any beat of any bar, so that you can work out the fingering, time, etc. at that particular point.

Sight-reading

Reading music at sight presents far less difficulty to some people (not always the most accomplished performers) than to others. Sight-reading piano or organ music (with the problem of co-ordination) is usually more difficult than reading a single stave at sight (e. g. violin, bassoon, or voice part).

The ability to read well at sight is a valuable accomplishment, and a sight-reading test is included in all grade examinations. Much can be done to improve the standard of sight-reading by careful and regular practice of suitable music. Books of graded sight-reading tests are published by the Associated Board, and other examining bodies. These provide excellent practice material, which becomes progressively more difficult with each grade. For the pianist, Béla Bartók's *Mikrokosmos* (Boosey and Hawkes), and Thomas A. Johnson's *Read and Play* series (Hinrichsen) are most valuable.

Sight-reading is primarily a matter of observation – the eyes take in clefs, time- and key-signatures, notes, accidentals, phrasing, dynamics, etc., and the fingers (feet, breathing apparatus, etc.) then make the appropriate physical response.

A special difficulty for the pianist (or organist) is to find notes on the keyboard without looking at the hands (the organist has also to find notes on the pedal-board without looking at the feet). On the piano keyboard this may be overcome by measuring distances between two notes, or the notes of a chord, with the eyes, and then trying to play them with closed eyes.

It is necessary to read as far ahead as possible, so that the grouping and phrasing of the notes is appreciated, and suitable fingering is used – this may, or may not, be indicated. The ear also plays an important part in sight-reading, and practice in singing melodies, and clapping rhythms, is especially useful.

Memory

The ability to memorise music varies greatly with the individual, and is not necessarily related to other kinds of musical skills. Memory implies two things: the capacity to retain knowledge, and the power to recall it.

Memory for music depends upon three forms of perception: visual, aural and tactile. Some people are gifted with 'photographic' memories, and are able to see a page of music in their mind's eye, and to reproduce it with complete accuracy. Others may find that music is easier to visualise if the shape is first concentrated upon, before dissecting it into sections. When the general shape has been memorised, the music can be analysed. Points to look for are firstly patterns of melody, harmony, rhythm, fingering, etc., secondly repeated passages, thirdly passages based on familiar figures, such as scale passages, *arpeggios*, etc., and fourthly sequences (see Glossary).

Aural perception may be developed by careful ear-training. The ear, like the eye, should take in the general design of the music, as well as the details. Tactile perception means that an instrumentalist is able to memorise the *feel* of the fingers as they play. The string player, for example, will note which fingers are closer together than others in particular passages, and where big stretches occur. The singer will not be concerned with tactile perception, but should learn to memorise the sensation which is felt when the right kind of tone is produced.

Nervousness often makes memorising difficult, and causes memory failure. Too much conscious effort may have the effect of paralysing the

Fig. 3
Ravi Shankar playing the sitar. He has given performances of classical Indian music in all the major cities of the world.

memory, and it is often better to play or sing music through without trying to memorise it, noting various points, and repeating it at intervals.

Mechanical aids

Listening to music on record, cassette, radio, television, etc., and taking careful note of speed, phrasing, dynamics, and so on, can be a helpful aid to study. Cassette tapes of music in the syllabus for grade examinations, and of the aural tests, are available, as well as cassettes dealing with intervals, harmony, form, composition, etc. Details from Hattrick Music Services, 33 Goodmayes Lane, Ilford, Essex IG3 9BB; Sound News Ltd, Hillier House, 509 Upper Richmond Road West, London SW14 7EE.

On some digital pianos guide lights are fitted over every key to show beginners which notes to play, and classical and popular piano music, including examination music and Christopher Norton's *Microjazz* (Boosey & Hawkes) recorded on floppy discs, can be played back in a variety of ways (e.g. at different speeds with the same pitch, and with either hand alone, allowing the pianist to play with the recorded music). For jazz players there are also 'play-along' recordings which enable players on any instrument to play with leading jazz artists and groups. Books with practice suggestions are included; videos of leading jazz performers are also available. Details from Jazzwise, 2b Gleneagle Mews, London SW16 6AF.

4

THE PIANO AND — EARLY KEYBOARD — INSTRUMENTS

── Early keyboard instruments ──

The piano as we know it is a comparatively modern instrument, but we may trace its origin at least as far back as the beginning of the 15th century. Each of the early keyboard instruments contributed something to the modern piano.

One of the earliest of the keyboard instruments is the clavichord, which dates from the 15th century. The clavichord is usually in the form of a shallow rectangular box without legs, which may be placed on a table for playing. The action of the keys is simple and direct; when a key is depressed, a brass blade (called a 'tangent') touches a string and causes it to vibrate. The tone of the clavichord is softer than that of other keyboard instruments; a gentle rocking motion of the finger on a key is used to create *vibrato** and expression.

The action of the virginals, spinet and harpsichord is quite different; a string is plucked by a plectrum made of quill or leather, which is fixed at right angles into a wooden 'jack' which rises when the key is depressed, and then falls back into position.

---

* Ger. *Bebung* (lit. 'shaking'). *Vibrato* on the clavichord produces minute fluctuations of pitch.

Virginals and spinets have one set of strings, with a jack to each string. Virginals are rectangular (or pentagonal) whereas spinets are wing-shaped or triangular. In the 16th century a small virginal was often placed on top of a larger one, thus providing the player with a 'pair of virginals'.

The harpsichord (It. *clavicembalo* or *cembalo*) is a much more elaborate instrument. Shaped rather like a grand piano, it often has two (sometimes three) keyboards, and several hand stops, or pedals, by means of which the player can vary the number of strings to a note, and also produce different kinds of sound (e.g. lute, harp, etc.). Despite its clear and incisive tone, the harpsichord is not able to sustain sounds to the extent of the piano, and the ornaments (turns, mordents, etc.) which abounded in the 17th and 18th centuries enabled the performer to prolong sounds, to some extent, especially in slow music.

In recent years there has been a strong revival of interest in early keyboard instruments, and modern reproductions are available, fully assembled or in 'kit' form. The harpsichord is used not only for the accompaniment of concerted music, such as that by Bach, Handel and other baroque composers, * but also for the performance of solo works by 17th and 18th century composers such as Couperin, Scarlatti, Bach, Handel, and some modern composers, for example *Harpsichord Concerto* (de Falla, 1926), *Concert champêtre* for harpsichord and orchestra (Poulenc, 1927–8), and *Continuum* for harpsichord (Ligeti, 1968).

The piano

The piano was invented by Bartolomeo Cristofori of Padua in Italy in about 1709, and the keyboard mechanism which he introduced laid the foundations of the modern piano action. In Cristofori's piano the felt-covered hammers which struck the strings were independent of the keys, and were lifted to the strings by pieces of wood called 'hoppers'. A device called an 'escapement' allowed the hammers to fall immediately from the strings, leaving them to vibrate. There was also a system of

---

* Baroque music for orchestra is usually supported by a *continuo*, a bass part with figures below it (hence *figured* bass) which indicate the harmonies to be played, or 'realised', on a keyboard instrument (usually the harpsichord); the bass part is also played by the viola da gamba or cello.

dampers which were raised when the keys were depressed, and fell as soon as the fingers were lifted, bringing the sound to an end.

Cristofori called his piano *gravecembalo col piano e forte* (harpsichord with soft and loud), from which we get the word pianoforte. (The earliest Italian name for the piano was *fortepiano*.) Cristofori's mechanism introduced an element of 'touch sensitivity' which it is not possible to obtain on the harpsichord (i.e. the greater the degree of force used in depressing a key, the louder the sound).

During the 18th century the piano action was modified and developed in Germany by Gottfried Silberman, in England by John Broadwood, and in France by Sebastian Erard.

The early piano had no pedals, and the power of sustaining tone was very limited. Sometimes levers were added which were controlled by the knees, and produced a *forte* effect by raising the dampers from the strings (like the sustaining pedal of the modern piano), and a *piano* effect by introducing a thin strip of cloth between the hammers and the strings.

The piano frame was at first made of wood but the strings, because of their thinness, were difficult to keep in tune. When they were made thicker the frame was braced with metal to withstand the increased tension. From about 1835, a cast-iron frame was introduced which allowed 'over-stringing', one group of strings passing diagonally over another group. The modern piano has one thick string, or two medium strings, to each of the lower notes, and three thinner strings to each of the remaining notes.

The compass of the piano was gradually extended. Cristofori's pianos had four or four-and-a-half octaves; today the piano usually has seven or seven-and-a-quarter octaves. Modern pianos are made either as uprights (full size or mini) or grands (several sizes from baby to concert). Older pianos were also made in shapes which included 'square' (oblong) pianos, and 'upright grands'.

The piano pedals

The modern piano has two pedals: on the right the damper, or sustaining pedal, on the left the soft pedal. A middle *sostenuto* pedal is also fitted to some pianos; this keeps some dampers raised while the pedal is depressed, but allows other dampers to fall. Modern pianos sometimes have a third pedal by means of which the tone can be muted for practising.

When the damper pedal is depressed it raises all the dampers from the strings (the shortest strings, having little power of sustaining tone, do not need dampers), so that notes which have been sounded continue to sound if the keys are released. The sounds are sustained until the damper pedal is released, or until the vibrations of the strings come to an end. The damper pedal also *enriches* the sound, for when one string is set in vibration with the dampers raised, other strings are free to vibrate in sympathy with it.

The soft pedal acts in one of two ways: on upright pianos the pedal, when depressed, moves the hammers nearer to the strings; on grand pianos it moves the keyboard and hammers to one side, so that where there are three strings to a note only two are struck, and where there are two, only one is struck. The soft pedal is used when a certain kind of tone-colour is wanted. Both pedals may be used independently or together.

The piano keyboard

The piano keyboard has a regular pattern of white and black keys – the white keys are at equal distances from each other whereas the black keys are grouped in twos and threes. This basic pattern is repeated throughout the entire length of the keyboard. Any two white keys which have a black key between them are a tone apart; two white keys without a black key between them (B and C, and E and F) are a semitone apart.

Section of the piano keyboard

Piano playing

There are many different methods of playing and teaching the piano, and many different opinions about the height of the piano stool, the position of the player's body and hands, etc. Piano technique has undergone many changes during the past hundred years, and innumerable theories have been advanced which have found favour for a time, and have then been superseded by fresh ideas. Exercises for strengthening and conditioning the fingers have been advocated, and mechanical devices have even been made for the purpose; Schumann lost the use of a finger through using a contrivance which he had invented.

Liszt (1811–86), though one of the world's greatest pianists, was responsible for a school of players who sometimes broke hammers and strings in an effort to get every ounce of available tone from the piano. Moscheles (1794–1870), a great pianist and teacher, advocated finger movement only, with completely still wrists, even suggesting that his pupils ought to be able to play with a glass of water balanced on each wrist!

Modern piano teaching is more influenced by Tobias Matthay (1858–1945) who wrote many books about his theories of relaxation and muscular control, and became one of the leading teachers in Europe. Another great pianist who founded his own method was the Pole, Theodor Leschetizky (1830–1915), whose pupils included Paderewski (1860–1941) and Schnabel (1882–1951).

The problems which confront the beginner at the piano, apart from note-reading, include the co-ordination of the right and left hands, an understanding of fingering and phrasing, and the proper use of the sustaining pedal.

The piano is a percussive instrument, and in smooth *legato* passages it cannot compete with instruments such as the violin or flute. Soft passages in particular need special efforts to reduce the percussive element to a minimum, keen aural perception, and an appreciation of the means of producing different qualities of tone. Broadly speaking, the piano keys are depressed by the exertion of the fingers or by the weight of the arm, or by a combination of both.

There are many excellent piano methods for the beginner; the teacher will doubtless suggest the most suitable one. Most methods begin with 'five finger groups' (i.e. consecutive notes which lie under the five fingers of each hand). After the first small pieces and exercises for each hand separately have been mastered, the problems of co-ordinating the two hands can be tackled. As well as learning to play pieces, scales and exercises will be introduced to strengthen and equalise the fingers. There should also be regular practice in sight-reading, and training in aural perception.

Music for the piano

The piano has a repertoire larger than that of any other instrument, and there is hardly any piece of music which has achieved popularity, which is not available as a piano arrangement. Although, next to the organ and electronic instruments, the piano is the most mechanical of all instruments, it is a medium for which most composers have written extensively.

Many of the great composers were themselves performers on the piano, or an earlier keyboard instrument, and the rich heritage of piano music includes the *Preludes and Fugues* of Bach, the sonatas and concertos of Haydn, Mozart, Beethoven and Schubert, and the piano works of Chopin, Schumann, Liszt, Brahms and Debussy, among many others.

Piano methods

Among the large number of methods relating to piano playing the following may be found useful:

Piano Lessons with Fanny Waterman and Marion Harewood (Faber Music)
A method, in several parts, which is excellent for the young pianist, and also for the adult beginner.
Me and My Piano by Waterman and Harewood (Faber Music)
For younger children (c. 6–8).
Mikrokosmos by Béla Bartók (Boosey & Hawkes)
A skilfully conceived series of pieces, in six volumes, covering a large number of the technical problems which confront the beginner and more advanced pianist.

Piano duets

Duet-playing is enjoyable, and provides useful practice in sight-reading and playing in time with another pianist.

Duet music is printed in one copy, with separate parts for each player. The first part (*primo*) is played on the upper part of the keyboard, and is

Fig. 4
W. A. Mozart (1756–91) at the keyboard, aged 6, with his father Leopold playing the violin.

often written in the treble clef for both hands. The second part (*secondo*) is played on the lower part of the keyboard, and sometimes the bass clef is used for both hands. The Primo part is usually on the right hand page, and the Secondo on the left; but sometimes the two parts are on the same page, one above the other. The Secondo player is usually responsible for the pedals, and often turns the page, though sometimes it is easier for the Primo player to do so.

There is quite a wide selection of piano duets, some with both parts of the same standard, and others with one easy part and one more difficult.

Some attractive duets include:

Two at the Piano, Waterman and Harewood (Faber Music)
50 short duets with the first part (easier than the second) progressing from simple five-note groups to independent parts for each hand.
Arcadia Book 1, Henk Badings (Schott)
10 duets by this well-known Dutch composer, in interesting modern style. The first part is easy, the second part more difficult.
Kathenka's Music-Book, Jurrian Andriessen (Broekmans and Van Poppel, Amsterdam)
5 very attractive pieces, with an easy first part (five finger groups), and a more difficult second part.
Nimble Fingers, Marjorie Helyer (Novello)
14 short duets with very easy parts for both pianists.
Microjazz piano duets, Christopher Norton (Boosey & Hawkes)
Four books of jazz duets; tuneful, and moderately easy (cassettes available).

———— Choosing a piano ————

A piano is a costly instrument, and the choice of one needs to be made with care. Pianos with famous names (such as Bechstein, Blüthner, Bösendorfer and Steinway) are likely to be beyond the means of most non-professional musicians, if they are in new or superb playing condition. Grand pianos are usually considerably more expensive than uprights, and the larger grands are not suitable for small rooms, although the smallest (baby) grands take up very little space. Uprights vary in size; the tone of the largest can be full and satisfying, but some of the smaller instruments are rather weak in tone.

Secondhand pianos are often advertised in musical journals and local newspapers, and a piano of a good make, which has been well maintained, may often be a better buy than a new instrument, although if a piano is old and has not been reconditioned, it is usually wise to have it examined by an expert, as the cost of restoring a badly neglected piano may be excessive. Defects such as worn or moth-ridden felts, warped hammers and dampers, rusty strings and worn keys should be looked for.

An overstrung upright piano is usually to be preferred to a vertically strung one, and an iron frame to a wooden one; and it is usually better for the dampers to be under the hammers rather than over them.

Looking after a piano

Unlike a fine violin, a piano does not improve with age. If played on regularly, the hammers and felts will develop deep ridges and will need to be renewed at some stage. The key-coverings (ivory or plastic) may also wear thin and will have to be replaced.

The position of the piano must be considered with care: it should not be placed in a draught (e. g. under an open window) or against a damp outside wall as damp can cause rusty strings, and warped hammers and dampers. Central heating may also cause problems which a humidifier may help to alleviate.

A piano needs to be tuned regularly by an experienced tuner who should be asked to keep the pitch up to standard (A = 440 cycles a second). If the piano is moved it will probably need to be retuned.

5

THE ORGAN FAMILY

Until the advent of electronic instruments, the organ family consisted only of the pipe (church) organ, the harmonium, the American organ, and a near relative, the piano-accordion. Today there is an infinite variety of electronic organs (and 'keyboards'), some small enough for home use and very easy to play, others suitable for churches and concert halls, and needing a considerable measure of skill.

The pipe organ

Pipe organs are built to individual specifications and vary considerably in size and detail, so that any description must necessarily apply to one particular instrument. The organ described below, from the point of view of the organist on the organ bench, is of moderate size and has three manuals.

In front of the organist is the *console* from which the three manuals rise one above the other. Each manual consists of a row of about 61 black and white keys, and looks similar to a piano keyboard, though shorter. The highest manual is called the *Swell*, and the pipes belonging to it are enclosed in a box with movable shutters. These can be opened or closed gradually by means of the *Swell Pedal* controlled by the organist's feet, thus producing an increase or diminution of the volume of sound. The middle and most important manual is the *Great*; the lowest is the *Choir*. Beneath the organist's feet is a large wooden keyboard (about two-and-a-half octaves) called the *pedal-board* or *pedal-organ*. Sometimes the console is situated some distance away from the organ, to which it is connected by an electric cable, so that the organist can more easily hear what he is playing, and be nearer to his choir, etc.

On both sides of the manuals (and sometimes above them) are rows of *drawstops* (handles which can be pulled out or pushed in). Some organs have *tabs* or *stop-keys* which can be flicked up and down, in place of drawstops. Each stop controls a complete set of pipes, all of which produce the same 'timbre' (tone-colour), and bears the name of that particular timbre and the length in feet of the longest pipe of the set. The pipes of an 8′ stop will sound at the actual pitch of the notes; those of a 4′ or 2′ stop will sound one, or two octaves higher, and those of a 16′ stop one octave lower. Each manual, and also the pedal-board, has its own set of stops, and until a stop is pulled out there will be no sound when a key is depressed. Above the pedal-board is a set of 'combination pedals', and by pressing these certain combinations of stops can be brought into use without raising the hands from the keys. On some organs the same result is obtained by pressing pistons which are placed beneath the manuals, and worked by the thumbs. The selection of suitable stops is called *registration*, and is an important part of the organist's skills.

There are several handles (closely resembling stop-handles) which are marked *coupler*, and are used to connect the stops of one manual with those of another. If, for example, the *Swell to Great* coupler is drawn the organist, playing on the Great, is able to combine any stops on the Great with any stops on the Swell, simply by drawing the appropriate stops on each manual. Another form of coupler is the *Octave* and *Sub-octave*, which enables a note to be played at normal pitch, together with another note an octave above or below.

The number and character of the stops on an organ is infinitely variable, but a three-manual organ of moderate size might include about six couplers, and thirty stops allocated as follows: ten stops each to the Swell and Great, and five each to the Choir and pedal organ. The Great is usually considered the most powerful manual, and is likely to have most of the diapason stops, a few flute stops, and perhaps a reed or two. The Swell usually has some quiet diapasons, some flute stops, and a fair selection of reeds. The Choir often has some attractive flute stops, as well as some quieter reeds.

Organ stops may be divided into groups, according to the quality of tone which they produce, although some stops may be felt to have the quality of more than one group. A 'stopped' pipe has a cover at the upper end which affects the tone quality (when compared to an open pipe of similar length).

Diapason tone

Produced from 'flue pipes' closely resembling the tin whistle, the diapasons represent the foundation tone of the organ, moderately full and somewhat assertive. Stops may include Fifteenth 2', Super Octave 2', Principal 4', Open Diapason 8', Stopped Diapason 8', Double Open Diapason 16'.

Flute tone

'Flute pipes', some of which may be stopped, or half-stopped, also produce flute tone. They 'speak' quickly, and are ideal for rapid passages. Stops may include Piccolo 2', Suabe Flute 4', Harmonic Flute 4', Claribel 8', Bass Flute 8' pedal stop.

Reed tone

Produced from pipes which incorporate brass tongues, or reeds, reed tone has considerably more edge and penetrating power than flute tone. Stops may include Clarinet 8', Oboe 8', Trumpet 8', and Trombone 16' pedal stop.

String tone

Produced from small scale flue pipes (scale = diameter of pipe at top), string tone is used for sonority rather than agility. Stops may include Gamba 8', Violine 8', Dulciana 8'.

Mixture stops

These are compound stops, with two or more pipes to each key.

Twelfth stop

This is a 2¾′ 'mutation' stop, sounding a twelfth above the actual notes. (Mutation stops produce sound at a pitch different from that which corresponds to a key which is depressed.) When added to other stops, mixture stops add brilliance, and mutation stops are useful for colouring the tone.

The 8′ stops are the most useful on each of the manuals. The mixture and twelfth stops are used in conjunction with 8′, 4′ or 2′ stops, to which they add a new tone-colour. The Voix céleste has two pipes to each note, one tuned a little sharper than the other. It is used with some other stop, such as the Echo Gamba, to which it adds a wavy, mysterious quality. The Vox humana is supposed to resemble the human voice, and is usually drawn in conjunction with the Tremulant (which produces an uneven flow of wind).

The fundamental differences between organ and piano technique have been discussed in Chapter 1. The organist may play with both hands on the same manual, or with each hand on a different manual. The art of organ registration is acquired by experience and careful listening. No description of the tone-quality of the stops can take the place of an aural demonstration. A balance must be achieved between the pedal-organ and the manuals by drawing appropriate stops on each.

The 8′ tone should be regarded as the basis of organ tone-colour, and should be used to accompany a solo stop. The pedals are often coupled to the manual on which the accompaniment is being played.

The effect of a *crescendo*, or more accurately the building up of tone, may be produced by gradually adding stops to soft 8′ foundation tone. The opposite effect may be produced by taking away stops one by one.

Single stops or stops of one family (Diapason, Flute, String or Reed) are preferable, as the frequent mixing of different stops soon becomes irritating. On small organs with few stops, variety of tone-colour may be obtained from time to time on 16′ or 4′ stops.

The pedal-organ has long and short keys, which may be compared to the white and black manual keys. The pedal-keys are played with the toe or heel, and are pressed down, not struck, by the movement of the ankle. In scale passages one foot is often passed behind the other.

Organ music is written on three staves, the top and middle staves for the manuals, and the bottom stave for the pedals. The repertory of the organ, though limited when compared to that of the piano, includes the incomparable organ works of Bach, Handel's concertos for organ and orchestra, and much noteworthy music by Rheinberger, Reger, Hindemith, Messiaen and many others.

———— The electronic organ ————

Although the tone quality of a full size electronic organ is bound to differ from that of a pipe organ (which is still found in most churches), the electronic organ has the advantage of taking up relatively little space. The initial cost is also less than that of a pipe organ of similar capacity, though the probable life span is considerably shorter.

There are several types of full size electronic organs. In the older type, the fundamental tones are produced by tone wheels which rotate close to a fixed electromagnet, or from a system of electrostatic generators, either rotating or vibrating. In other types the tones are generated by transistors (or valves); transistorised organs have the advantage of remaining in tune if there is a voltage drop in the mains supply. The sound comes from loudspeakers in different parts of the church or room. The technique of a full size electronic organ is similar in many respects to that of a pipe organ, and it may thus be a useful practice instrument when a pipe organ is not available.

With the advent of the computer, a new dimension was added to the electronic organ. One of the larger models, the Allen Digital Computer Organ, has 48,000 minute computers giving limitless tonal possibilities. The main computer, the 'specification memory', contains tonal information for the 36 stops of the two-manual instrument. An electronic card-reader is added to some models, so that when computer cards are placed into either the Swell or Great division, hundreds of extra stops are made available.

On some electronic organs it is possible to record music at a slow speed and replay it at a faster speed. Unlike pipe organs, which need tuning from time to time, most electronic organs will stay in tune almost indefinitely, although the pitch as a whole may be made sharper or flatter by the adjustment of a control.

——————— The reed organ family ———————

The sound of instruments in the reed organ family is produced by the pressure of air on thin metal tongues known as *free reeds*, which move in and out of an air-slot without completely closing it.

The harmonium has the same manual compass as the pipe organ (five octaves), and the music is written on two staves like piano music. There is usually a row of ten stop-handles, of which eight bear a number and two are blank. Each numbered stop-handle acts on a different set of reeds. The blank stop-handles are the *Grand Jeu* and the *Expression stop*. The Grand Jeu brings all the stops into action at the same time, so that the full power of the instrument is heard. The treadles provided for the feet feed the bellows, the wind thus created being stored in a reservoir which must be kept regularly supplied with air. The Expression stop, when pulled out, allows the air to act directly on the reeds by cutting off this reservoir. The tone may therefore be increased or decreased by blowing more or less strongly. There are two octave-couplers similar to those on the pipe organ, and a tremulant device. Below the keyboard are two wooden flaps called knee swells – when pressed outwards the right-hand flap produces a *crescendo*; the left-hand one gradually brings all the stops into action, cancelling them as it is released.

The technique of the American organ is similar to that of the harmonium, with one or two exceptions. The smaller instruments have only six stops, the stop-handles bearing names, and figures showing the length of the stops in feet. There is no Expression stop. Some of the largest American organs have two or more manuals and a pedal-board, the technique being like that of the pipe organ.

——————— The piano-accordion ———————

The piano-accordion consists of pleated bellows with piano-type keys for the right hand, and buttons for the left hand which produce bass notes and simple chords. There are usually 120 buttons, i.e. 40 bass notes and 80 chords, but sometimes there are as few as 12 or as many as 210. The free metal reeds are activated by the compression or expansion of the bellows. There is also a *free bass accordion*, with an additional, or alternative, keyboard of single notes for the left hand, which allows the player to play bass melodic passages instead of pre-set chords.

There are miniature accordions suitable for children, and also an electronic version without reeds and bellows, but fully transistorised and reproduced by an amplifier and loudspeaker.

6

THE SINGING VOICE

Singing is, or should be, a natural process. Some people are born with voices which develop into instruments of beauty and power, without much formal training and study (e.g. there are many 'natural' voices among the Welsh people). Most people, however, do need careful training if the voice is to reach its full potential.

There are many so-called methods of voice training, and a singing teacher needs to be chosen with care. Much can be done to develop the quality of a voice and to enlarge its compass, but in the hands of an inexperienced teacher, who fails to classify the voice correctly and tries to progress too quickly, damage to the vocal cords can result, which may be irreversible.

Developing the voice

The technical equipment of a singer is twofold: the ability to produce a full and beautiful tone, and to pronounce words distinctly and correctly.

The voice, the only natural musical instrument in existence, is built on principles similar to those of an organ reed-pipe. The reed-pipe has a metal reed, which produces sound when it is made to vibrate; the voice has two tiny elastic strips of cartilage, each about 1.25 cm (½ in) long, known as 'vocal cords', which act as sound-producing reeds when breath is passed between them. The sound produced by the reed of the reed-pipe, or by the vocal cords of the voice, may amount to little more than a squeak; the pipe itself, and the mouth and nasal cavities, act as resonators, developing the squeak into full and vibrant tone.

The vocal cords act automatically. The singer imagines a sound, and the vocal cords assume the correct tension to produce it. It is easy, of course, to imagine a wrong, or out of tune, note, but apart from this the singer does not worry about the action of the vocal cords, so long as he realises that they must vibrate freely and must not be strained by forcing the voice.

Unfortunately the breathing and resonating apparatuses do not function entirely automatically, and the singer must give some thought to them. Since the mouth and nasal cavities act as resonators, the quality of sound is conditioned by the shape of the mouth, and this depends on the position of the lips, tongue, soft palate (the fleshy substance which forms the back part of the roof of the mouth), and lower jaw.

The sensation of directing the vocalised breath in such a way that it strikes against a particular resonator is called 'placing' the voice. Thus the voice may be directed forward or backward, or to the middle. If *ah* is sung, followed by *oo*, the sensation will be of the sound leaping forward from the back of the throat to the lips. Forward tone, such as that produced when placing an *m* or *n* before a vowel, is the most useful for the beginner to practise, because the untrained voice has a natural tendency to become throaty.

The compass of the voice may be extended by the practice of scales and exercises, starting with a range of about an octave-and-a-half (or even an octave or less), and adding a note at a time at each end of the voice. A soprano, for example, might start by practising from D (above middle C) up to G (an octave and three notes higher). This is only a generalisation; the development of the voice is an individual matter, and few definite rules can be given. The deciding factor must always be whether or not notes can be produced naturally and without strain.

—— Classification of voices ——

No two singers' vocal organs are exactly alike, and no two voices have exactly the same compass and sonority of sound. But in a general classification of voices there are four main divisions: soprano, contralto, tenor and bass, subdivided into mezzo-soprano and baritone. In classifying voices, both compass and vocal quality have to be considered.

Female voices are classified as the following.

Soprano

The highest voice, divided into three classes:

1 **Dramatic soprano:** powerful, especially suited to the performance of 'declamatory' music which depicts anger, excitement, rapture or other strong emotions.
2 **Lyric soprano:** lighter and more agile than the dramatic soprano; the most usual form of soprano voice.
3 **Coloratura soprano:** with a bright, penetrating flute-like quality, a high compass, and an ability to sing quick passages with great agility, and to perform vocal acrobatics.

Mezzo-soprano

The commonest of female voices, combining the brightness of the soprano with the richness of the contralto; it has a full, mellow, flexible tone.

Contralto

The true contralto voice is rare; it has a rich, heavy quality which, though less flexible than that of higher voices, is capable of greater expression.

Male voices are classified as the following.

Tenor

The highest voice, divided into two classes:

1 **Light or lyric tenor:** brilliant, flexible, the male counterpart of the lyric soprano.

2 **Heavy or robust tenor:** full, vigorous, corresponding to the dramatic soprano.

Baritone

The commonest of male voices, midway between tenor and bass; more flexible than the bass, and deeper than the tenor. There are light and heavy baritones, the light voice having more of a tenor quality than the heavy one.

Bass

The deepest male voice, divided into two classes:

1 **Basso cantante or lyric bass:** sometimes called bass-baritone, with qualities similar to those of the other lyric voices.
2 **Basso profundo or deep bass:** most powerful voice with the lowest compass.

Male alto or counter-tenor

This 'falsetto' (head) male voice, which has nearly the compass of the female contralto voice, was especially cultivated in England for use in church music during the 16th and 17th centuries. It continued during the 18th and 19th centuries, and more recently there has been a revival of interest in the falsetto voice for the performance of early music, and in some modern works (e.g. the character of Oberon in Britten's *A Midsummer Night's Dream* (1960) is played by a counter-tenor).

Children's voices

During childhood, boys and girls have much the same voices. At puberty the boy's vocal cords rapidly lengthen, and after a period during which the voice is said to be 'breaking', it settles down an octave or so lower than before. The girl's voice also alters, but the change is more gradual and less noticeable. It is generally accepted that boys and girls who have been singing from an early age may continue to do so in a quiet way during adolescence. It is usually inadvisable to begin serious training before the age of seventeen or eighteen.

Vocal quality

Since the classification of voices is conditioned not only by compass but also by quality, a singer who has the compass of, say, a tenor voice cannot be considered a tenor unless his voice is of tenor quality. It is not unknown for the quality of the voice to change completely during its development, and several well-known singers have started their professional careers as tenors and changed to baritone, or vice versa.

Music for voices

Music for female voices is written in the treble clef, but male singers should have a knowledge of both treble and bass clefs. When the treble clef is used for the male voice the notes are written an octave higher than they actually sound.

The average compass of each voice is:

Example 75

Words

Song is a combination of two arts, music and poetry. Ideally, each should complement the other, but however skilfully the composer may blend them together the ultimate responsibility for keeping them in this state falls on the performer.

In singing, vowel sounds are often sustained considerably longer than in speech, and the singer must learn to pronounce them correctly. The pure sounds of the vowels should not be sacrificed on the grounds of expediency, simply to facilitate tone production.

Diphthongs, in which two vowel sounds are made into one, need special care. *OI* as in *joy*, for instance, is formed from *AW* and *I* (as in *it*). *I* (as in *lie*) is formed from *AH* and *EE*. When diphthongs are sung the first vowel sound must be sustained, and the second made as short as possible, so that the common error of pronouncing *light* as *lah-eet*, and *joy* as *joy-ee*, is avoided.

General indistinctness of speech in song is often caused by failure to articulate consonants. 'Light and love' often becomes 'ligh tan love'. In correcting this we must not go to the other extreme and sing 'light*er* and *er* lov*er*'. We may compromise by pronouncing each final consonant in a whisper, audible but not obtrusive.

Consonants such as *P* and *B*, and *D* and *J*, are often confused – we get '*b*owerful' for '*p*owerful', and '*d*ew' for '*j*ew'. *P* and *B* are formed with closed lips; *P* is more explosive than *B*, and needs to be articulated more crisply. *T* and *D* are formed with the tip of the tongue. *J* and *Z* are articulated with the middle of the tongue. *R* is trilled (rolled) by the tongue, except when it comes at the end of a word. Consonants such as *B, G* and *D* are often wrongly preceded by a kind of buzzing sound: *ur*bee, *ur*gee, *ur*dee. *S* and *X* need special care to avoid hissing.

Breathing

Breathing consists of two acts – breathing in and breathing out. In singing, sounds have often to be sustained, so breathing must be deeper than in speech. The difficulty is not so much in taking in sufficient breath as in knowing how to use it. Breath is the motive power of the voice, and the singer has to learn not to waste it, but to translate it into sound.

In simple terms the process of breathing may be described thus. Breathe in slowly, steadily, silently and deeply, as if inhaling the fragrance of a rose. As you breathe imagine that you are about to yawn, and the throat will assume the 'open' position. When breathing out, imagine that you are sighing deeply.

When breathing, the singer must have regard to the phrasing of the music. A fresh breath should normally be taken where there is a slight pause in the words; this will usually coincide with a punctuation mark. Sometimes it will be necessary to take a 'half-breath' (when only a little breath is taken in), or to snatch a breath (e.g. during a long Handelian run which is vocalised on a vowel sound).

Choral singing

Choral singing, whether in church choir, choral society, operatic society or other group, is enjoyable and excellent practice. A trained voice is not always necessary, and a singer will gain confidence from hearing other voices, and given a good chorus master or conductor will learn a great deal about singing and music in general. Choral singing is easier than solo singing so far as technique is concerned, but the singer who wishes to become a useful member of a well-established choral society should devote some time to sight-reading, as many large classical and modern works will probably be performed during the year.

The most important thing in choral singing is unanimity, which means that all the voices must attack and release a note, and swell and diminish the tone, exactly together. This unanimity must also be applied to words, and everyone must be in agreement about the pronunciation of difficult words.

Choral music is usually written in four parts, for soprano, alto (i.e. contralto), tenor and bass (SATB for short); the mezzo-sopranos sing with the sopranos, and the baritones with the basses.

Four-part choral music is often written on two staves (i.e. in 'short score'), the notes of the upper parts on each stave having their stems turned up, and those of the lower parts having their stems turned down (Example 76). In short score, the tenor part is written in the bass clef, the notes sounding at their actual pitch.

When choral music is written on four staves (i.e. in 'open score', Example 77), the tenor part in the treble clef sounds an octave lower than written; to indicate this a small 8 is often written under the clef sign.

When choral music is sung without accompaniment, the balance of the

Example 76

Handel

See the ⎯ con - qu'ring he - ro comes,

Example 77

See the ⎯ con - qu'ring he - ro comes,

See the ⎯ con - qu'ring he - ro comes,

See the ⎯ con - qu'ring he - ro comes,

See the ⎯ con - qu'ring he - ro comes,

voices becomes of extreme importance. (It. *a cappella* 'in the church style' is often applied to choral music for unaccompanied voices.) Ideally, each section of the choir should be perfectly proportioned – in a choir of forty singers, for example, there might be thirteen sopranos, eight contraltos, eight tenors, and eleven basses. But since contraltos and tenors are rarer than sopranos and basses, they will seldom be apportioned in this way, except in professional choirs; there will probably be too many sopranos and too few contraltos and tenors. Good balance must then be obtained by grading the tone so that the weaker sections are not overwhelmed by the stronger ones, or by borrowing voices from one section to add to another. The standard of balance must always be the strength of the weakest part.

7

STRINGED, WOODWIND, BRASS AND PERCUSSION INSTRUMENTS

Stringed instruments

'String' is a term which is usually applied to instruments which are played with a bow; not, therefore, to the guitar, mandolin, harp, lute, etc. The modern string family consists of violin, viola, cello and double bass; there is an earlier family of viols of different sizes.

The compass of the modern string family is as shown in Example 78 below.

Example 78

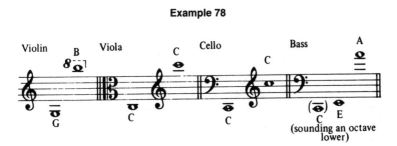

Higher notes are possible with first-class players.

Violin

The modern violin first came into use in Italy during the early 16th century. In the city of Cremona the Amati family, and later the Guarneri and Stradivari families, made violins which have never been surpassed; those Cremonese instruments which have survived are highly prized for their tone and construction. There were many imitators, some excellent, some indifferent. Thousands of violins bear the label of a famous maker, but this usually indicates the model which the instrument follows, rather than the name of the maker. There are also many fine old instruments by French and British makers.

Choosing a violin is no easy task and, unless there is someone who can give an expert opinion, it is better to be guided by an instrument dealer of repute, who will offer good advice. The real test of a violin is the tone, which should be sweet, full and pleasing to the ear, and of a uniform quality throughout its compass. Violins (and also cellos) are made in small sizes (half, quarter, etc.) for children.

The violin consists of a wooden sounding-box formed by two surfaces called the belly (made of soft wood such as pine), in which two holes resembling the letter ∫ ∖ are cut, and the back (made of hard wood such as sycamore), which are united by the sides or ribs. A neck, ending in a curved scroll, is attached to the sounding-box, and an ebony fingerboard to the neck. The strings, which pass over the belly of the instrument, are fixed at one end to an ebony tailpiece, and at the other end to movable pegs by means of which the pitch may be raised or lowered. The strings are raised from the belly by a small wooden bridge, which is supported by a small wooden sound-post placed in the interior of the instrument. The bridge is curved, so that the bow may be drawn across each string without coming in contact with the others.

The bow consists of a stick, made of hardwood, such as Brazilian lance wood or pernambuco, with horse hair stretched over it, and attached to an ebony head (called a 'nut' or 'frog) which may be made to slide to and fro by turning a metal screw at the straight end of the bow, thus tightening or loosening the hair. The stick of the bow is cut straight, and afterwards bent by subjecting it to heat which gives it a springy quality.

Before playing, the hair of the bow is adjusted so that it is moderately tight, but not so tight as to pull the stick out of shape, and is lightly drawn across a block of resin to increase the grip. When not in use the hair is loosened so as to relieve the stick of any strain.

The hair of the bow, under a microscope, has tiny teeth like those of a saw. When these wear away after much playing the hair must be renewed by a competent firm of repairers. A bow used for an hour a day may need new hairs every few months. The strings of the violin are tuned in perfect fifths, as shown in Example 79 below.

Example 79

| 4th string | 3rd string | 2nd string | 1st string |

G   D   A   E

Formerly the E, A and D strings were gut, and the G string gut covered with wire. Nowadays the E string is usually wire, and sometimes also the A and D strings, or gut covered with wire. Wire strings last longer than gut ones, and keep in tune better. When they are used, a little appliance called a 'string adjuster' is often fitted to the tailpiece to enable fine adjustments to be made.

The use of the bow   The bow, held lightly between the four fingers and thumb of the right hand, is drawn firmly across the strings, with the stick somewhat inclined towards them, so that the hair is turned towards the bridge. The stroke of the bow from heel (held by the hand) to point is called 'down bow'; that from point to heel 'up bow'. The stroke may either be changed for each note, or several notes may be played in one stroke. When notes are played smoothly in one stroke they are said to be 'slurred', and the bowing is called *legato*; this is one of the most useful and charming strokes on the violin. Change of direction of the bow is shown by the signs ⊓ (down bow) and ∨ (up bow).

Staccato bowing may be 'on the string' (i.e. notes played in a short, crisp manner), or 'off the string' (*spiccato*), when the bow is dropped on to the string, and rebounds.

The *martelé* (or hammer) stroke is often used when a strong accent and firm tone are needed. This stroke is played at the point of the bow, by pressing the hair firmly on the string, and then playing with a quick, elastic pressure of the wrist.

Fingers   The fingering of modern stringed instruments played with a bow is based on the fact that if a string is 'stopped' by the fingers (i.e.

made shorter by pressing it down on the fingerboard) the pitch will be raised. A string that is not stopped is said to be 'open' – the use of an open string may be shown by the sign 'o' placed over or under a note. The four fingers of the left hand are used for stopping notes; the thumb, of course, is not available. The different fingers are shown by placing figures 1, 2, 3 or 4 over or under notes.

If the first finger is pressed down on the 4th (G) string, a small distance up the fingerboard, it will (if correctly positioned) stop the note A; the second finger placed a similar distance from the first will stop B; and the third finger, placed a *smaller* distance from the second, will stop C. The fingers, placed in the same positions on the 3rd (D) string will stop the notes E, F sharp and G, so that the scale of G major may be fingered thus:

Example 80

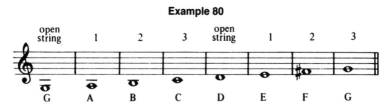

The second and third fingers are placed closer together than the first and second fingers; the reason is that B to C and F sharp to G are semitones, whereas A to B and E to F sharp are tones.

The fingers, if placed in the same positions on the 2nd (A) string will stop B, C sharp and D; on the 1st (E) string they will stop F sharp, G sharp and A. The fourth finger on the G string, placed a small distance from the third finger, will stop D, the same note as the next open string. This means that the D above middle C can be produced either on the G string or on the open D string. Similarly, the open string notes A and E can also be produced by stopping the string below with the fourth finger. There is, of course, no open string above the E string; the fourth finger on it will stop B.

If the first finger is pressed down on the G string to stop the note A, and is then moved back a little way, it will stop G sharp. Similarly, if the third finger is moved farther away from the second finger it will stop C sharp instead of C natural. By moving fingers backwards and forwards in this way, a chromatic series of notes may be played. (In the 20th century it has been customary to use an individual finger for each semitone (open, 1, 2, 1, 2, 3, 4, open).)

G	G sharp	A	A sharp	B	C	C sharp	D
Open G	1	1	2	2	3	3	Open D
string							string

It will be seen that by using the fingering so far given, a complete chromatic scale can be played, extending from open G string to B (fourth finger on E string). It is possible, however, to extend the upward compass beyond B, and to provide many alternative ways of fingering on all strings, by moving the hand up the neck of the violin (towards the bridge) in a series of shifts, or 'positions'. If, for example, the hand is shifted a little way up from its normal position (called the first, or natural, position), the first finger on the E string will stop G instead of F sharp, and the fourth finger will stop C instead of B. If the hand is shifted about 2.5 cm (1″) farther up, the first finger will stop A, and the fourth finger D.

The skilled player will use ten, or even twelve positions to obtain notes on the highest (E) string. Positions above the fifth are seldom used on the first three strings. Example 81 shows the notes which can be played in the first five positions on the A string.

Example 81

The fingers of the left hand must be trained to fall firmly and smartly on exactly the right part of the strings, otherwise the notes will not be in tune. Hence the need for a discriminating ear. Scale practice and exercises will strengthen the fingers and make them supple.

Tone production The production of a clear singing tone is the most difficult part of violin playing; the foundations of tone are best laid by drawing long, straight bows. The bow should be held lightly (though firmly enough to control it), and the tone should be produced with a light pressure of the wrist. Scales can be practised for tone production by playing each note with a full bow, as slowly as possible.

Further points of technique If a string is touched very lightly at certain points, and not pressed down on the fingerboard, it will produce high sounds of a light, flute-like quality. These are called 'natural harmonics', and are shown by placing an **o** over the notes which are to be lightly touched. If a string is firmly stopped with the first finger and lightly touched with the fourth, an 'artificial harmonic' will be produced, sounding two octaves higher than the stopped note. This is indicated by writing the note to be stopped as an ordinary note, and the note to be touched as a diamond-shaped note a fourth higher.

Two notes on adjacent strings may be played at the same time to form a chord. The simplest chords are those played on two adjacent open strings (G and D, D and A, or A and E). Chords may also be formed by playing two stopped notes on adjacent strings, or one stopped note and one open string. Any two-note chord is usually called a 'double-stop', even if both notes are on open strings.

Three-note chords (triple-stops) and four-note chords (quadruple-stops) may also be played. When playing a three-note chord, the bottom and middle notes are attacked together (usually before the beat), then the middle and top notes are attacked and sustained. In a four-note chord the two lowest notes are attacked together, then the two highest notes are sustained.

The word *pizzicato* (It. 'plucked') means that notes so marked are to be plucked with the finger, instead of being played with the bow. The resumption of bowing is shown by the word *arco* (It. 'bow').

Sometimes a small three-pronged *mute*, made of wood or metal, is placed on the bridge of the violin, and has the effect of attenuating the sound to a kind of silvery whisper. The use of the mute is shown by the Italian *con sordino*; the contradiction is *senza sordino*.

The repertoire of the violin is large, and includes music written, or transcribed, by virtuoso violinists such as Tartini (1692–1770) famous for his *Devil's Trill* sonata, Paganini (1782–1840), Spohr (1784–1859), Vieuxtemps (1820–81), Wieniawski (1835–80), and Kreisler (1875–1962). There are many duets for two violins (including easy ones), and also trios for three violins.

Viola

This was a neglected instrument, and up to about the 18th century it was mainly used to double some other part in the orchestra. Even later, when the viola developed some sort of individuality, the standard of playing was low. Because it was seldom given important music, it was considered easier to play than the violin, and was often taken up by second-rate violinists who were anxious to make quicker progress.

Later still, under Lionel Tertis (1876–1975) and other distinguished players, the viola acquired some of the dignity it deserved, but it has always suffered from the smallness of its repertoire.

The viola is tuned a perfect fifth below the violin:

Example 82

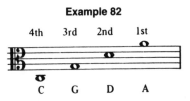

Music for viola is written in the alto clef, with occasional use of the treble clef for high passages. The tone has a veiled quality; it is sometimes rather nasal, but on a large instrument (there are various sizes) it is rich and penetrating. The technique is the same as that of the violin, except that there is a slightly larger stretch between the fingers on the fingerboard, because of the lower pitch. Apart from this, all the principles of violin technique apply to the viola, and any violinist should be able to transfer to the viola quite easily.

The instrument should be carefully selected and strung, as the viola is more likely to have defects of tone than the violin. Some violas have one or two 'wolf' notes, which are heard as two notes, perhaps a quarter of a tone apart, sounding at the same time. The two lowest strings (C and G) are both made of gut covered with wire, and sometimes, after much use, the covering may work loose, causing a string to rattle when played on. It must then be replaced.

A special bow is used by most players, but some prefer a full-size violin bow of rather heavy design.

Cello

The cello is a fine solo instrument and, next to the violin, the most useful member of the orchestra. Its repertoire is fairly large, and includes many trios for piano, violin and cello. It is no more difficult to learn than the violin. The cello is made in full, three-quarter, half and quarter sizes. In appearance it is like a large violin, except that it has a long metal 'peg' which is used as a support, and which is slid into the body of the instrument when not in use. The cello is pitched an octave below the viola, and is tuned in perfect fifths:

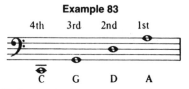

Example 83

Although the cello is considerably larger than the violin, the bow is shorter, though heavier, so that in *legato* passages bow direction is changed more frequently than on the violin.

Cello technique differs from that of the violin in some aspects, although both instruments have many principles in common. The cello is held by gripping it between the knees, the right knee being lowered so that it is out of the way of the bow. The direction of cello bowing is the reverse of violin bowing, the cello bow pointing towards the string. In the lower positions, cello fingering differs from that of the violin because of the greater distance between notes on the fingerboard. The cellist may stretch a semitone between any two adjacent fingers, and a tone between the first and second fingers, but not between the second and third, and third and fourth.

Cello fingering is therefore less regular than that of the violin; the scale of C major, one octave ascending from the open C string, can be fingered thus:

C		D	E	F	G		A	B	C
Open string		1	3	4	Open string		1	3	4

The hand is moved up the neck of the cello for the various positions, as on the violin. In the higher positions fingering is more like that of the violin. Cello music is written in the bass clef, but the tenor and treble clefs are used for higher passages.

Double bass

This is the largest instrument in the string group and is normally used only in an orchestra or dance band, since it is too unwieldy for solo purposes. It has, however, been used in a few chamber works, such as Schubert's *Trout* quintet (1819) for violin, viola, cello, double bass and piano, and Koussevitsky (1874–1951), a famous double bass player and conductor, wrote a double bass concerto. The double bass is similar in appearance to the cello except for its sloping shoulders. In the 19th century three-stringed basses were in favour, but the modern instrument usually has four strings tuned in perfect fourths:

Example 84

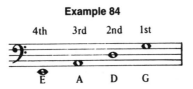

Most double basses are fitted with an attachment which extends the compass to low C. The music is normally written in the bass clef, but the tenor clef may be used for high passages – the music is written an octave higher than it sounds. The fingering of the bass, in the higher positions, is like that of the cello. In the lower positions the maximum stretch is a tone between first and fourth fingers, and a semitone between first and second.

The double bass player should be fairly tall as the instrument stands about 1.82 m (6 ft) high, and have strong fingers as the strings are thick and heavy to press down.

Viol family

The family, or consort, of viols was widely used in the 16th and 17th centuries, often for playing concerted music for from three to six viols. There was wide variation in sizes and shapes, but a 'chest of viols' often consisted of a set of six instruments in three sizes: two trebles, two tenors and two basses. Viols have six strings, tuned to intervals of a perfect fourth, with a major third between the two middle strings. The fingerboard has gut *frets*, giving a clear sound to the stopped notes. The bow is held above the palm of the hand, and all viols are held vertically either between the knees or resting on them. The name *viola da gamba* (It. 'leg viol') was later applied to the bass viol, which was often used as a solo instrument for playing 'divisions' (variations) on a ground bass (a bass part constantly repeated, with varied upper parts). The bass viol was also used extensively for playing the bass line in continuo parts (see the footnotes on page 69).

In modern times there has been a revival of interest in the viol, and modern viols are specially made for the performance of early music.*

Guitar

The modern Spanish or classical guitar has six nylon strings, the 4th, 5th and 6th springs being overwound with fine wire. By means of metal screws called machine heads, the guitar is tuned thus:

Example 85

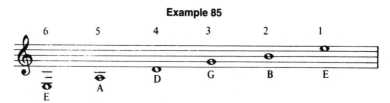

The player is seated with the left foot resting on a footstool, the guitar being supported between the right knee and the left thigh, with the right elbow resting on the side of the instrument. The strings are plucked with the fingers of the right hand. The neck of the guitar forms a fingerboard to which frets, spaced a semitone apart, are fitted, Notes are stopped by placing the fingers of the left hand directly behind the frets.

Guitar music is normally written an octave higher than the actual sounds, so that only the treble clef is needed. When playing popular music, a small piece of horn, ivory, etc. (called a plectrum) is sometimes used for plucking the strings. Written compass:

Example 86

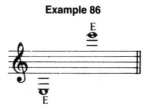

---

* Details of modern makers of viols, baroque wind instruments, harpsichords, etc. may be found in *Early Music*, published quarterly by Oxford University Press.

Because of its relatively weak tone, the guitar is often fitted with steel strings and electrically amplified, for folk, country and western, and rhythm playing. The cost of an electric guitar is normally higher than that of a non-electric (acoustic) one. The steel-string guitar is often played in a standing position, the instrument being supported by a neck cord.

There is also a four-string electric bass guitar, tuned like the double bass, which it often replaces in popular combinations. Bass guitar music is written in the bass clef, an octave higher than the actual sounds.

Lute

The history of the lute dates back to about 200 BC, and this plucked instrument has been made in many shapes and sizes. The body of the lute is shaped like a half-pear. There is a fretted fingerboard, and a pegboard which is bent back at an angle.

The 16th century lute had 12 strings arranged in courses (i.e. pairs of strings plucked together to give more volume). There were several different methods of tuning the strings.

In the 16th and 17th centuries the lute was widely used as a solo instrument and for song accompaniment, and many lute books of this period have been preserved. There has been some revival of interest in the lute, with its delicate, expressive tone, and modern lutes are made for the performance of period music, some in 'kit' form.

Mandolin

The mandolin, the most recent member of the lute family, is chiefly to be found in southern Italy. The eight wire strings of the Neapolitan mandolin are tuned in courses to the same notes as the strings of the violin. The strings are plucked with a plectrum, usually with a backwards and forwards *tremolo* motion, so that the sounds can be sustained.

The mandolin is chiefly used to play popular melodies, but it appears at times in the music of serious composers, such as Mozart's *Don Giovanni* (1787), Verdi's *Otello* (1887), and Mahler's 7th symphony (1904–5).

Electric mandolins have been made which enhance the volume.

Banjo

The banjo, of American Negro origin, has a shallow circular metal body which is covered with parchment at the top and open at the bottom, and a long neck. Banjos have been made with from four to nine strings, and are played with the fingers, or with a plectrum. The four-string tenor banjo was part of the rhythm section of the early dance band, but was later superseded by the guitar. The banjo, once very popular in 'minstrel' shows, is still occasionally used in several forms including the banjo-mandolin, and the guitar-banjo, with six strings tuned and played as a guitar.

Wind instruments

The technique of the various wind instruments will be described briefly, and some general principles outlined. Further information can be obtained from the books and methods mentioned on page 243.

Woodwind instruments, broadly speaking, are based on the same principles as those of the tin whistle: six holes bored in a tube, which are covered and uncovered by the fingers to produce different notes. If these holes are uncovered one by one, the notes of the major scale can be produced, and the intermediate semitones, or some of them, can be obtained by *cross-fingering* (i. e. by covering a hole below the one which is sounding). Then by using the same fingering and blowing harder, the same series of notes may be produced an octave higher. Even so, there are gaps in the scale, as well as imperfect notes, because there are not enough fingers to control all the holes that ought to be bored in the whistle to produce a perfect chromatic scale. After numerous attempts to fit keys to wind instruments to facilitate the fingering, a system was devised by a Munich flute-player, Theobald Boehm (1794–1881), whereby holes could be cut in the proper positions, and yet be easily opened and closed by the fingers. The essence of the 'Boehm system' is that four holes come under the control of three fingers. All modern flutes are designed on this system, and also, with slight modifications, oboes and clarinets. When buying an old instrument it is important to bear this in mind.

Flute

The compass of a modern flute is as follows:

Example 87

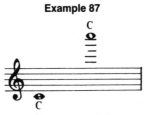

Two additional top notes (C sharp and D) are also possible in *forte* passages. Exceptionally, some flutes are made with a low B. The instrument as we know it today is made up of three pieces:

1 **The head,** which is more or less conical, and is plugged at one end with a cork or 'stopper', and in which is cut the mouth-hole or *embouchure*. The embouchure is partly covered by the lower lip of the player, who directs his breath *across* it, so that it strikes the opposite edge.

2 **The body,** a cylindrical tube which carries the system of keys which are manipulated by the fingers of the player.

3 **The foot joint,** which is added to allow the two bottom semitones, C and C sharp, to be produced.

The fingering for each octave is much the same, and the upper octaves are produced by 'over-blowing' (i.e. by increasing the wind-pressure), which brings the harmonics into action, instead of the fundamental sounds.

The modern flute is usually made of metal. The tone-colour varies considerably at different parts of the compass. The lowest octave has a thick, velvety tone, which is rather easily covered up by other instruments. The middle octave is smooth and limpid, somewhat resembling the voice of a boy singer. The top octave is brilliant and penetrating, the two highest semitones being very difficult to play softly. Rapid passages and trills are easy and effective. When nimble passages are played, double- or triple-tonguing is often used. When tonguing in this way, the player, by articulating T-K and T-K-T, is able to play a succession of *staccato* notes with the utmost ease and rapidity.

The flute repertoire contains sonatas and solo pieces by Bach, Handel,

Haydn, Mozart and Schubert, and by a number of modern composers, as well as some chamber music for flute with other instruments. As a solo instrument the flute is charming, and well suited to an average-sized room. In the orchestra it is frequently given important solo passages.

The concert piccolo, or octave flute, is pitched an octave above the concert flute, and its music sounds an octave higher than the written notes. The written compass is the same as that of the flute, except that the two lowest semitones are not available. The lower notes of the piccolo are weak, but the higher notes are shrill and penetrating. The second (or third) flute player in an orchestra often plays both flute and piccolo, as the technique of both is similar.

Oboe

The oboe consists of a conical tube, expanding at the lower end into a bell. The tube is usually made in three sections: the upper and lower joints and the bell. The double reed, from which the sound is produced, consists of two thin strips of cane fastened to a small metal tube or 'staple', so that a tiny space is left between them. The normal compass is as below.

Example 88

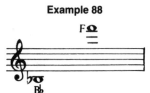

Some players can reach notes a few semitones higher. The tone, in the hands of a good player, is penetrating but sweet, equally charming in *legato* and *staccato* playing. Tone production is more difficult than on the flute or clarinet. The reed is placed between the lips, which cover the teeth and form a sort of cushion, and the beginning of every phrase is 'attacked' by placing the tongue against the reed, and then withdrawing it to allow the breath to pass. This is called 'single-tonguing', the only kind of tonguing which can be used on the oboe, because of the position of the reed in the mouth.

The management of the breath usually presents some difficulties. The player must take in just sufficient breath to play each phrase, and often a quick half-breath must be taken in the middle of a phrase.

The reed of an oboe is very delicate and great care must be taken not to damage it, as a fine tone can only be obtained when the reed is in perfect condition. Many players make their own reeds, an operation requiring some skill and a few special tools, as ready-made reeds are not always to be relied upon.

The cor anglais, or English horn, is pitched a perfect fifth below the oboe. In the orchestra it is usually played by an oboe player, and for this reason its music is always written a perfect fifth higher than it sounds, so that it may be read without difficulty, using the same fingering as that of the oboe. The written compass is the same, except that the lowest semitone (B flat) is missing. The cor anglais is longer than the oboe, and ends in a globular bell. The reed is placed in a metal crook which is bent back to meet the player's lips. The tone is smooth and rich, and peculiarly adapted to melancholy music. The fingering and technique is the same as that of the oboe.

The oboe repertoire, though small, contains some attractive solo pieces, a number of concertos with orchestra, and some chamber music. There are a few solo pieces for cor anglais, which also has a part in some chamber works.

Clarinet

The clarinet is descended from a medieval instrument called the 'chalumeau', a name applied to the lower register of the clarinet, but the modern type of clarinet did not come into regular use until about Mozart's time.

It is a single reed instrument consisting of a mouthpiece, a cylindrical tube, and a bell. The tube, not being conical like that of the flute and oboe, overblows a twelfth instead of an octave.

There is thus a gap between the octave and the twelfth which is filled in by a system of fingering which is not entirely satisfactory. This part of the compass, therefore, is rather dull and lifeless. The lower notes have a rich, oily quality but the upper part of the compass is best, since it is clear, even and expressive. The clarinet has great agility (it replaces the violin in the military band), and has greater powers of playing *pianissimo*, and of swelling and diminishing the tone, than any other wind instrument.

The orchestral clarinettist uses two instruments, one pitched in B flat and the other in A. The written compass for both is as shown overleaf.

Example 89

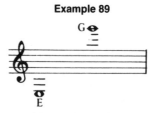

Music for the B flat clarinet sounds a tone lower than written; music for the A clarinet sounds a minor third lower than written. Thus, if the note C is written, it will sound as B flat on the B flat clarinet, and as A on the A clarinet. The fingering and technique of both instruments is the same, so that the player can change from one to another without difficulty. If only one instrument is purchased, the B flat clarinet should be chosen, as it is the more useful of the two. The bass clarinet in B flat is pitched an octave below the ordinary B flat instrument, and the written compass is the same. Because of the great length of the tube, the lower end is curved upwards in the shape of a bell, and the upper end is curved inwards to bring the mouthpiece nearer to the player's mouth. The reed of the clarinet is a flat piece of cane, held to the mouthpiece by a metal clamp called a 'ligature'.

Before purchasing a clarinet method or tutor, it is necessary to make sure that the system is the same as that of the instrument.

The clarinet has a fairly large repertoire of solo pieces, concertos, and chamber music.

Bassoon

The compass of the bassoon is shown below:

Example 90

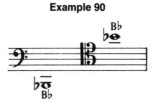

Bassoon music is written in the bass and tenor clefs. The long tube is made in two sections which are united at the lower end, and the double reed is fixed to a curved metal tube. The tone is reedy and powerful, and the bassoon's natural function is to provide the bass of the woodwind group. As a solo instrument it is capable of producing comic effects and for that reason it used to be called 'the clown of the orchestra'. The limited repertoire includes a number of solo pieces and concertos, as well as chamber music.

The double bassoon is a large and ponderous instrument with a heavy and obtrusive tone. Its music is written an octave higher than it sounds and the written compass ends a perfect fifth below that of the bassoon. In the symphony orchestra it is usually played by the second or third bassoon player, and is used for reinforcing the low notes of the woodwind group.

Recorder

This end-blown flute, which was very popular in the 16th, 17th and 18th centuries, went out of fashion until it was revived early in the 20th century, largely through the efforts of Arnold Dolmetsch, and is now very popular in schools.

The modern recorder, which has a whistle mouthpiece, is made in five sizes which together form a 'consort', or family of recorders. The compasses are as follows:

Example 91

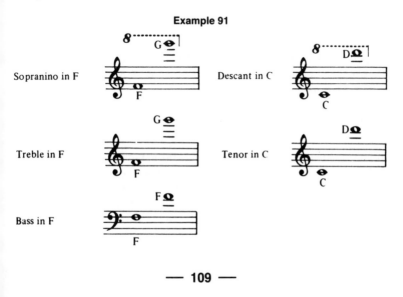

— 109 —

Of these, the treble is the most useful as a melody instrument, although the descant is popular, especially for use in schools. The sopranino, which is an octave above the treble, has a charming tone, but its use is limited. The quiet tone of the tenor makes it less suitable for solo performance. The bass is large (and fairly expensive), and is less easy to play than the other recorders. It is, however, an extremely useful addition to the consort. The recorder's repertoire is quite large, ranging from medieval and renaissance music (both solo and ensemble) to music by 20th century composers.

Saxophone

The saxophone, though made of metal, is a conical-bored instrument of the woodwind type, and has a reed and mouthpiece similar to those of the clarinet. The tone is thick, and rather obtrusive. Its written compass is as follows:

Example 92

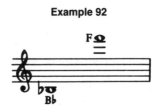

Saxophones, though used extensively in dance and military bands, are not often found in the symphony orchestra, though they have been used with excellent effect by some composers (e.g. Mussorgsky-Ravel, *Pictures from an Exhibition* (1922); Walton *Façade* (1923), Vaughan Williams, *Job* (1930).

Although saxophones are made in seven sizes, the most useful are:

Name	*Sounds*
Soprano in B flat	A tone below written notes
Alto in E flat	A major sixth below written notes
Tenor in B flat	A major ninth below written notes
Baritone in E flat	A major thirteenth below written notes
Bass in B flat	Two octaves-and-a-tone below written notes

For general purposes the E flat alto and B flat tenor saxophones are the most widely used. In light combinations saxophone players often double on clarinets.

Infrequently used woodwind instruments

These instruments have been used by a few composers in individual works; in the symphony orchestra they are usually doubled by the second or third woodwind player of the appropriate section. Examples of works in which these instruments are to be found are given on page 119.

Alto flute in G   The written compass (sounding a perfect fourth lower) is as follows:

Example 93

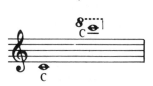

This is sometimes incorrectly called the bass flute. Because of its larger size, the notes are richer than the corresponding notes of the normal flute; the lower notes are especially characteristic.

Oboe d'amore   The written compass (sounding a minor third lower) is as follows:

Example 94

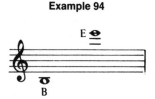

This instrument, which was in common use in Bach's day, is pitched midway between the oboe and the cor anglais. The tone is sweeter and more gentle than that of the oboe.

Heckelphone (Bass oboe)   The written compass (sounding an octave lower) is shown overleaf.

Example 95

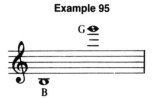

The heckelphone is 1.21 ms (4 feet) long, with a short metal support which rests on the floor. The bore is wide, and the reed of the bassoon type.

The bass oboe has the same compass, but a less weighty and penetrating tone than that of the heckelphone. It sounds much like the cor anglais, which it resembles in shape except that the crook bends forwards and then backwards towards the player.

E flat clarinet This small clarinet, which is used in the military band to reinforce the top octaves, is occasionally found in the orchestra. The tone is more shrill and penetrating than that of the ordinary clarinet. Its written compass (sounding a minor third higher) is as below:

Example 96

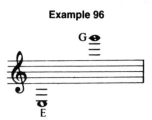

Basset horn This is a clarinet in F (a major third lower than the clarinet in A); the part is normally written a perfect fifth higher than the actual sounds. Basset horn parts are normally written in the treble clef. If the bass clef is used, the parts are written a perfect fourth below the actual sounds. Although the basset horn has the same bore as that of the A or B flat clarinet, in appearance it is more like the bass clarinet. The written compass (sounding a perfect fifth lower) is as follows:

Example 97

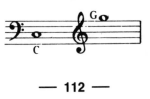

Contrabass clarinet   Large clarinets have been made in B flat to sound an octave below the bass clarinet in B flat. They have also been made in E flat.

Sarrusophone   This instrument, which has occasionally been used in the orchestra, was invented by Sarrus, a French bandmaster, towards the end of the 19th century. It is made of brass, but is played with a double-reed similar to that of the bassoon. It has the same written compass, but sounds an octave lower.

Early woodwind instruments

Many examples of woodwind instruments of the 16th century exist, and modern replicas are made for the performance of early music. (Trinity College of Music has a department of Renaissance and Baroque Music, where early string and wind instruments may be studied.) There are contemporary tutors and descriptive books by writers such as Agricola (1486–1556), and Praetorius (c. 1571–1621). The oriental system of classifying instruments as loud or soft was adopted by the West. Loud instruments performed in outdoor activities, while soft instruments were heard at indoor functions and on quieter occasions.

16th century music which was composed for voices was also performed by consorts of instruments of different sizes. These were either members of the same group, or a mixture of two or more groups. There were consorts of flutes (treble, tenor and bass), and of crumhorns, cornetts, curtals and shawms. The basic fingering of these instruments was similar to that of the recorder, though there were different cross-fingerings. Originally each set of instruments was made in three sizes, each size corresponding to the voice parts of a composition, so that the performer could change from one to another, reading the same notes, and fingering them, so far as possible, in the same key. Other sizes (e.g. descant and great bass) were later added to the consorts.

The crumhorn, which was particularly favoured as a consort instrument, is made of boxwood, with the lower part bent round. It is played with a double reed (somewhat similar to the bassoon reed) which is enclosed in a cap with a hole at the top through which the performer blows. The cornett (not to be confused with the cornet) is a long, thin tube of wood or ivory, covered with leather, and can be either straight or curved. The sound is produced through a cup mouthpiece. The curtal is the earliest form of bassoon, and the shawm is the forerunner of the oboe.

Brass instruments

Brass instruments are based on a completely different system from woodwind instruments. We have seen that a violin string, if lightly touched at certain points, will produce a series of weaker sounds called *harmonics* or *partials*, which are normally unheard unless they are made prominent. The vibrating body (string or tube) vibrates not merely as a whole to produce the lowest (fundamental) note, but also in halves, thirds, quarters, and so on. If we suppose a string or tube with the fundamental note two octaves below middle C, the following series can be obtained:

Example 98

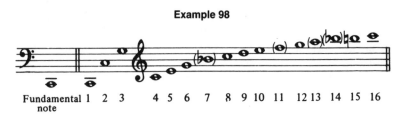

Nos. 7, 11, 13 and 14, which are enclosed in brackets, are slightly out of tune. Different brass instruments use different sections of the harmonic series, according to the length of their tubes, and individual harmonics may be brought into prominence by the lip action of the player.

Gaps between harmonics are filled in by using valves or pistons (French horn, trumpet, cornet, tuba), or by manipulating a slide (trombone). The effect of either device is the same: the tube is lengthened, and the pitch is consequently lowered. The trumpet, cornet and French horn are provided with three pistons, or valves; the tuba has a fourth piston. When each piston is depressed, an additional small piece of tubing is added to the main tube, and when the piston is released the extra tubing is cut off. One piston lowers the pitch of the entire harmonic series by a semitone, another by a tone, and a third by a tone-and-a-half. Two or three pistons may be used together; for example, the tone and the tone-

and-a-half pistons will lower the pitch by two-and-a-half tones, and all three pistons will lower it by three tones.

The trombone has a sliding tube which may be placed in seven positions, so that the harmonic series may be lowered in six stages of a semitone; the third position is a semitone below the second, etc.

The tuba has special difficulties of pitch, and the fourth piston can lower the pitch a perfect fourth.

The horn

The French horn is a coiled tube, narrow at one end and expanding into a large bell at the other. A funnel-shaped mouthpiece is inserted into the narrow end. The double-horn, used by most professional players, has two sets of tubing operated from the same three valves. A fourth valve enables the player to switch from the F horn to the higher B flat horn, and vice versa, thus making the highest notes less difficult to produce.

Horn music is written in the treble (or sometimes the bass) clef, a perfect fifth above the actual sounds. When, on the double-horn, the player chooses to use the B flat section, he must employ a new set of fingerings. The written compass (sounding a perfect fifth lower) is as follows:

Example 99

Sometimes, in order to get a certain quality of tone, the hand is inserted into the bell, and the notes so produced are said to be 'stopped'. A mute placed in the bell gives a somewhat similar effect.

The normal tone may be mellow or brassy, according to the action of the player's lips. Tone production requires great skill as the player must 'feel' the notes before he can produce them and, until he can do this instinctively, he will often find himself 'wobbling' off the note.

Before the application of valves to horns and trumpets, it was only possible to play the notes of the harmonic series, so that the player had a very limited number of notes at his disposal. To overcome this difficulty the natural horns and trumpets were provided with a number of *crooks* – pieces of tubing of various sizes which could be changed according to the key of the music.

The trumpet and cornet

The modern trumpet is pitched in B flat or C; the B flat instrument may be put into A (but seldom is), either by pulling out a sliding tube, or by turning a tap which automatically includes or shuts off an additional piece of tubing. Its written compass is shown below:

Example 100

This sounds as written on the C trumpet, a tone lower on the B flat trumpet and a minor third lower on the A trumpet.

The cornet in B flat has the same compass as the B flat trumpet, but is shorter and tubbier. It is used in military and brass bands, and occasionally in the orchestra.

Both the trumpet and cornet use a cup-shaped mouthpiece though the cornet mouthpiece is deeper than that of the trumpet. Cornet technique is much easier to acquire than trumpet technique because the cornet 'speaks' more easily, and the notes can be produced with greater certainty. Cornet tone is more mellow and less brassy than trumpet tone. Double- and triple-tonguing are possible on both instruments. The tone of the trumpet (and cornet) can be modified by inserting a mute in the bell; several kinds of trumpet mutes are used, particularly in jazz and popular music.

The trombone

Three trombones are normally used in the modern orchestra: two tenors in B flat and one bass in F. The tenor trombones are written in the tenor and bass clefs, and the bass trombone in the bass clef. Their compasses are shown below:

Example 101

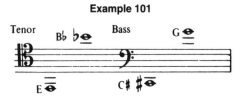

A bass trombone in F (compass C to F) is often used, and there is also a tenor-bass trombone having the combined compass of the B flat and F instruments.

Owing to the slide action, a true *legato* is not possible. The mouthpiece is cup-shaped and is held to the player's lips by the left hand, which also supports the instrument. The slide is controlled by the right hand, either by a wrist or an arm movement. The bass trombone slide is so long that a jointed handle is fitted to allow it to be fully extended. Like the trumpet, the tone of the trombone may be modified by the addition of a mute; several kinds of mutes are used in the jazz orchestra.

Tuba

The orchestral tuba in F is similar in appearance to the heavy brass basses which are to be found in military and brass bands. The tuba has a conical tube, widening into a large bell, and is played with a wide cup-shaped mouthpiece. Its compass is shown below:

Example 102

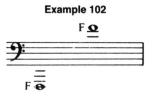

In the orchestra the tuba is usually associated with the trombone, for which it provides a firm bass. Despite its rather heavy and obtrusive tone, the tuba can be surprisingly agile. It can be muted, but this is exceptional.

Although the brass instruments are mainly used in the orchestra, the horn and the trumpet have a small repertoire of solo pieces, concertos with orchestra, and chamber music. One of the few solo works for the tuba is the concerto by Vaughan Williams (1954).

Infrequently used brass instruments

Examples of use are to be found opposite.

Trumpet in D　This is a small valve trumpet which is sometimes used for playing notes which would be uncomfortably high for the larger trumpets. The written compass is the same as that of the C and B flat trumpets, but the actual sounds are a major second higher than written. The trumpet in D, which may be converted into E flat sounding a minor third higher than written, is also used when playing high trumpet parts by Bach and Handel.

Bass trumpet　The bass trumpet varies in shape and size. It is fitted with three or four valves, and in some forms it is virtually a small valve trombone. When pitched in C or B flat, the written compass is the same as that of the usual trumpet in C or B flat, and the part is usually in the treble clef, sounding an octave lower than the written notes. A bass trumpet has also been made in E flat. The part is written in the treble clef, and sounds a major sixth below the written notes.

Flügel horn　This is a valved bugle, similar to the cornet in appearance, but with a wider bore and larger bell. The tone is more horn-like than that of the cornet. The flügel horn in B flat has the same compass and pitch as the B flat cornet. Flügel horns of different sizes (called saxhorns) have been used in some European orchestral music.

Tenor tuba, euphonium　Parts for the tenor tuba in B flat are usually played on the euphonium, a small tuba with three or four valves which is a regular member of military and brass bands. Its normal compass is shown below (the note in brackets is the lowest on the four-valve euphonium).

Example 103

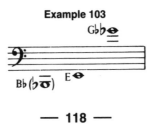

Although composers usually write for the tenor tuba (or euphonium) in the bass clef at actual pitch, Richard Strauss has written for the tenor tuba in the bass clef, a tone above the real sounds, and Holst has written in the treble clef, a major ninth above the real sounds.

Infrequently used wind and brass instruments

Examples of orchestral works in which these instruments are to be found:

Alto flute: Holst, *The Planets* (1915); Ravel, *Daphnis et Chloe* (1912); Stravinsky, *The Rite of Spring* (1913).

Oboe d'amore: Ravel, *Bolero* (1928).

Heckelphone: Richard Strauss, *Salome* (1905), and *Elektra* (1909).

Bass oboe: Holst, *The Planets* (1915).

E flat clarinet: Berlioz, *Fantastic Symphony* (1830); Ravel, *Bolero* (1928); Britten, *Peter Grimes* (1945).

Basset horn: Richard Strauss, *Der Rosenkavalier* (1911).

Contrabass clarinet: Schoenberg, *Five Pieces for Orchestra* (1909).

Sarrusophone: Ravel, *Rapsodie espagnole* (1907); Delius, *Eventyr* (1917).

Saxophone: Bizet, *L'Arlésienne* suites (1872); Berg, Violin concerto (1935).

Cornet: Elgar, *Cockaigne* overture (1901); Stravinsky, *Petrushka* (1911).

Trumpet in D: Stravinsky, *The Rite of Spring* (1913); Ravel, *Bolero* (1928).

Flügel horn: Vaughan Williams, 9th symphony (1958).

Tenor tuba (or *euphonium*): Holst, *The Planets* (1915); Richard Strauss, *Don Quixote* (1897).

Wagner tubas: There are five in all, four of which are of a special type, designed to be played by horn players. Few orchestras possess these instruments, though they were also used by Bruckner (7th symphony (1881–3) and Richard Strauss, *Elektra* (1909).

——— Percussion instruments ———

There are two groups of percussion instruments – those of definite pitch and those of indefinite pitch – and each is dealt with below.

Instruments of definite pitch

Timpani   The timpani (kettledrums) consist of large basins of copper or fibre-glass over which heads of calf skin or plastic are stretched. The heads are fastened to wooden hoops held in place by iron rings which may be raised or lowered by means of either hand-screws or pedals. The heads may thus be tightened or slackened, and the pitch raised or lowered. The modern pedal timpani and the older hand-tuned drums have the same range and tone-quality, but whereas any alteration of pitch can be affected almost instantaneously with pedal timpani, time must be allowed if the drums are hand-tuned.

Timpani sticks have flexible handles, and heads of soft, medium or hard felt, sponge or other material. For special effects, wooden (or side drum) sticks may be specified, and these need to be handled with care, to avoid damaging the drum heads.

Until the early 19th century timpani were traditionally used in pairs, a small drum being tuned to the tonic, and a larger drum to the dominant. The average compass of the small drum was B flat to F, and of the larger drum from F to C. Thereafter a third drum began to be used, and the average compass of the three drums, from largest to smallest, was E flat to A flat, G to D, and C to G. Modern music for timpani is written in the bass clef as it sounds, and four or more drums are often found in the professional orchestra. The usual compass of four drums is shown below:

Example 104

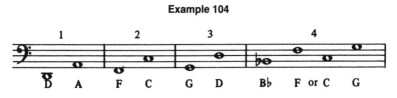

Whereas the older timpani were tuned by means of tensioning screws, the modern pedal mechanism enables changes of pitch to be made with great speed and accuracy. The handling of pedal timpani does, however, require an exceptionally accurate sense of pitch.

Antique cymbals   These miniature cymbals, made of brass or some other alloy, were used by dancers some 2000 years ago. There are various kinds of antique cymbals; those known as 'crotales' are usually of definite pitch, whereas 'antique' cymbals may be of definite or indefinite pitch. 'Finger' cymbals are, in theory, of no pitch. Antique cymbals were introduced by Berlioz into *Romeo and Juliet* (1839), and have been used by later composers (e.g. Debussy, *Prelude à l'après-midi d'un faune*, 1894).

Tubular bells   Orchestral bells are usually tubular, since the church-tower type would be far too cumbersome. The tubes are hung from a rack, and struck near the top of the tube. The chromatic range varies, but in Europe and America one-and-a-half and two octaves sets are available. The compass of a one-and-a-half octave set is shown below:

Example 105

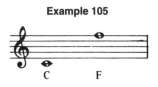

C   F

Glockenspiel   This is a set of little metal plates laid out in two rows, chromatically, and struck with light beaters of wood or rubber. Single notes and simple melodic figures are best suited to the instrument. The tone is clear and fairy-like, and when hard beaters are used it is quite penetrating. The average compass is shown below:

Example 106

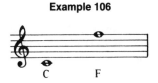

C   F

The glockenspiel usually sounds two octaves higher than the written notes; but sometimes one octave higher (e.g. Wagner, *The Master-singers*, 1868). Occasionally the glockenspiel is fitted with a small keyboard (e.g. Lambert, *The Rio Grande*, 1929), but such instruments are not often in use today.

Xylophone   This consists of graduated bars of hard wood, usually arranged in two rows on a frame. Tuned resonators are often fitted beneath the bars. Several kinds of beaters are used, of wood, rubber or felt, each producing a different quality of sound. By using two hammers in one hand, chords of from two to four notes can be played. Rapid *staccato* passages, repeated notes, and *glissandos* (rapid continuous movements up or down the scale) are easy and effective. The average written compass (sounding an octave higher) is shown below:

Example 107

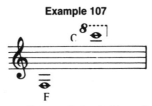

Marimba   In appearance the marimba is like a large-sized xylophone, though the tone is warmer and less brittle, and is thus better suited for expressive melodies. The marimba is pitched an octave below the xylophone. The usual compass is four octaves, starting from the octave below middle C. The marimba is more often used in light combinations than in the symphony orchestra, though Milhaud wrote a concerto for marimba and vibraphone (1947).

Vibraphone   This electrical development of the glockenspiel is found mostly in light and dance orchestras, though it has been used on occasions by serious composers (e.g. Britten, *Spring Symphony*, 1949). Like the glockenspiel it has steel bars which are struck with hammers. Under each bar is a tuned resonator, at the top of which a small metal disc is fitted. These discs are made to revolve by means of an electric motor, thus causing the sound to pulsate. A damper pedal enables the sound to be stopped or sustained. Slow melody notes, and single chords of up to four notes, are well suited to the rather cloying sweetness of the floating tone. The written compass is shown below:

Example 108

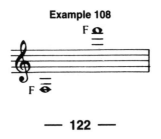

Cimbalom   This Hungarian instrument consists of metal strings (two or more to each note) fixed to a wooden frame and struck with spoon-shaped sticks. The sounds may be dampened by means of a foot-pedal. Its usual written compass is shown below:

Example 109

Celesta   The celesta, which was invented by Mustel in Paris in 1886, consists of small steel bars fitted with wooden resonators, and struck by felt-covered hammers controlled by a keyboard similar to that of the piano. A pedal is also fitted to increase the sustaining power of the instrument. The clear tone has an ethereal quality, and is mainly used for decorative purposes against a soft background. Its written compass (sounding an octave higher) is shown below:

Example 110

Examples of its use are Tchaikovsky, *Nutcracker Suite*, 1891–2, and Bartók, *Music for Strings, Percussion and Celesta*, 1936.

Instruments of indefinite pitch

Snare drum (side drum)   This was originally a marching drum, which the player carried at his side. The modern snare drum consists of a wooden or metal shell, and heads of calf skin or plastic with a diameter of about 35.6 cm (14 in), and a depth of about 15.2 cm (6 in). The upper head only is played on, and across the lower head some eight to twenty strings (snares) of gut, nylon, wire, etc. are stretched, giving the drum its characteristic rattle. If the snares are loosened (by releasing a lever), the rattle disappears and the drum sounds rather like a tom-tom. The drumsticks are made of hardwood, with small oval-shaped ends. Whereas the roll on the timpani is produced with alternate single strokes, the snare drum roll is made with double alternate strokes with each hand (nicknamed 'daddy-mammy'). The skill to produce a smooth roll, and the other strokes, requires much practice.

Tenor drum   A larger and deeper version of the snare drum, with a diameter of about 45 cm (18 in), and a depth of about 30.4 cm (12 in). In countries other than Britain it is also sometimes snared.

Tabor   A long, narrow drum popular in the Middle Ages, with one or two heads, with or without a single snare. There is a part for tabor in the Farandole from Bizet's *L'Arlésienne* (1872), often mistakenly played on the tambourine.

Bass drum   This large drum has one or two calf skin heads, and a deep tone which can be atmospheric (*pp*) or powerful (*ff*). The single-headed drum is known as the *gong drum*. The drum is struck with a large wooden stick, padded at one end to form a ball of felt. A roll can be performed with a double-ended stick, or with timpani sticks.

Cymbals   These are two thin metal plates in the centre of which are raised domes with holes through which leather hand straps are inserted. When clashed together loudly with a swinging movement, they produce a shattering sound which adds intensity to points of climax. After being struck, the cymbals can either be allowed to vibrate, or can be damped, by pressing them against the player's body. *Pianissimo* effects may be obtained by touching very lightly, or gently rubbing together. A lighter sound is obtained when one cymbal is suspended, and struck with a snare drum or timpani stick.

Triangle   A steel rod bent into triangular shape which, when suspended by a string and struck with a metal beater, produces a clear, bell-like sound of indefinite pitch.

Castanets   Two small round pieces of hardwood, hollowed out in the centre, which are clicked together in various rhythms. For orchestral use they are often mounted on a wooden handle.

Gong (Tam-tam)   The orchestral gong is a large round plate made of hammered bronze, with the edge turned over. It is suspended by a cord, and struck with a large soft-headed beater. A heavy blow produces a powerful crash, a soft blow a mysterious, sinister sound. The tam-tam, one of the largest gongs, is of indefinite pitch, whereas some of the smaller gongs have a definite pitch (e.g. Puccini uses a set of tuned gongs in *Turandot*, 1926).

Wood block   A rectangular block of wood, in which slits are cut to form a resonating cavity. Snare drum sticks, or xylophone mallets, are used to play single notes or simple rhythms. The tone is hard and dry, and is often used for comic effects.

Temple blocks (Chinese temple blocks)   A series of wooden blocks, hollowed out from a slit in the centre in the shape of a fish. They are played with wooden or felt sticks, and the tone might be described as a 'glop'. There are different sizes (most drummers have at least three) and the pitch, though indefinite, varies according to the size.

Rattle (Ratchet)   Occasionally used as a percussion instrument, the sound is produced by tongues of flexible hardwood striking against a cog which is turned in a hand frame.

Sleigh bells (Jingles)   A set of small metal bells each containing a steel ball. They are normally fastened to a leather strap, which is often fixed to a wooden handle, and is jogged by the hand.

Whip (Slapstick)   The effect of a crack of a whip is produced by striking together two thin narrow pieces of wood. It is played with both hands by means of the straps or handles attached. The slapstick is of a different design and is played with one hand only – its two wooden pieces are fitted with a spring and a handle.

Tom-toms   Tom-toms are snareless double- or single-headed drums. There are two kinds; either pitchless or tuneable. They are usually in sets of from two to eight, and chromatic sets are available. Another kind of tom-tom, the tuneable *rototom*, is fitted with a timpani head and is also widely used.

Anvil   This is supposed to reproduce the sound of a blacksmith's anvil. Although anvils have been used they are extremely heavy, and substitutes are often used to produce a similar effect. Wagner's *Rheingold* (1869), and Verdi's Anvil Chorus in *Il Trovatore* (1853) make use of anvil effects.

Wind machine   This consists of a large cylinder of wooden slats, which when turned by a handle comes in contact with a canvas covering which is stretched over a wooden frame. The intensity of the wind sound depends on the speed with which the cylinder is rotated. It is used by Richard Strauss, *Don Quixote*, 1897, and *Alpine Symphony*, 1915, and Michael Tippet, *4th Symphony*, 1976–7.

Latin-American percussion instruments

Percussion is the basis of all Latin-American dance music, and some of the percussion instruments have also been used in more serious compositions. Among the Latin-American instruments are the following:

Claves   Two short sticks, which are struck together to produce sharp cracks (e.g. Copland, *Appalachian Spring*, 1944).

Maracas   Hollow gourds with handles, containing dried seeds or beads which rattle when the gourds are shaken (e.g. Varèse, *Ionisation*, 1933).

Bongos   A pair of small Cuban drums with single heads. They are held between the knees and played with the fingers (e.g. Varèse, *Ionisation*, 1933).

In the rumba, conga, bolero, etc., claves, maracas and bongos play a basic rhythm, other percussion instruments being added as required. The following are characteristic rhythms:

Example 111

— 126 —

Guiro (Fr. râpe guero)   A notched gourd which is played by scraping the notches with a small stick. It is used for slower dances, such as the bolero (e.g. Stravinsky, *The Rite of Spring*, 1913).

Harp

The modern double-action harp, which was perfected by Sebastian Erard in the early 19th century, is tuned to the diatonic scale of C flat, each octave having seven strings, C, D, E, F, G, A and B, all flats. Seven pedals are provided, each of which, when depressed into either of two notches, brings discs fitted with pins into contact with certain strings, thus 'stopping' them and raising the pitch. Each pedal affects all the strings of a particular letter name. Thus, the C pedal, when pressed halfway down (first notch) raises all the C flat strings a semitone to C natural or, when pressed farther down (second notch), a tone to C sharp. Each string may therefore be raised a semitone or a tone without changing its letter name – the reason, of course, for tuning the harp in the basic key of C flat. Since each string is associated with its letter name, C sharp would be played on the C string, and D flat on the D string, even though they have the same sound. By using the appropriate pedals, the harp can thus be set in any key, but since a chromatic scale would involve very frequent changes of pedal it is out of the character of the instrument. On the other hand, once the pedals are set to a particular chord, that chord may be repeated throughout the compass of the instrument, simply by drawing the fingers across the strings. The harp has therefore almost unrivalled powers of *arpeggio* and *glissando* playing.

Harp music is written on two staves, using the treble and bass clefs, as in piano music. Its compass is shown below.

Example 112

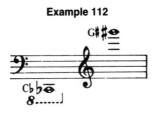

7a

SELF-TESTING QUESTIONS

1 Transpose this passage for the instruments named, using the appropriate key-signature.

   (a) Cor anglais   (d) Horn in F
   (b) B flat clarinet   (e) Trumpet in A
   (c) E flat alto saxophone (f) Guitar

2 Give the meaning of the following:
   (a) *pizzicato*   (d) double-tonguing
   (b) *con sordino*   (e) double-horn
   (c) plectrum   (f) gong drum

3 Which modern instruments are played with a double reed?

4 In which basic key is the harp tuned?

5 Name five different members of the recorder family.

6 Which drums can produce sounds of definite pitch?

7   Which two instruments of the modern string family are tuned to the notes C, G, D, A?

8   Which metal instrument has a reed and mouthpiece similar to those of the clarinet?

Answers can be found on page 240.

8

THE MODERN ORCHESTRA

The full complement of the symphony orchestra of today is usually from eighty to one hundred or more players. There are four main groups of instruments: woodwind, brass, percussion and strings. This is the order in which the instruments appear in the full score, in which the parts to be played by each instrument are written systematically on staves one above the other, to provide the conductor with a complete view of the music. The harp does not fall into any of the four groups and, when used, appears immediately above the string group.

— The constitution of the orchestra —

The exact combination of the modern symphony orchestra varies according to the works which are to be performed. An orchestra of about one hundred players might consist of:

Woodwind 3 flutes (3rd doubling piccolo)
3 oboes (3rd doubling cor anglais)
3 clarinets (3rd doubling bass clarinet)
3 bassoons (3rd doubling double bassoon)
Brass 4 horns (sometimes 5, 6 or 8)
3 trumpets
3 trombones (2 tenor and one bass)
Bass tuba

Fig. 5
The City of Birmingham Symphony Orchestra with Simon Rattle, principal
conductor, in Symphony Hall.

Percussion	Timpani (3 or more drums, played by one or more players). Other percussion (one or more players, playing side drum, bass drum, cymbals, triangle, xylophone, glockenspiel, etc.)
Harp	One player (sometimes two). (Wagner's *The Ring of the Nibelung* (1869–76) requires six harps.)
Strings	18 first violins
	16 second violins
	14 violas
	12 cellos
	10 double basses

This orchestra of about one hundred players contains a large proportion of strings (70). Normally, all the first violins (18) will play the same part (though on occasions they may be divided into two or more parts). The same applies to the second violins, violas, cellos and double basses. This large body of strings forms the backbone of the orchestra, and provides versatile orchestral sound with a characteristic smoothness and sonority.

In contrast each member of the woodwind and brass usually plays an individual part, though on occasions some instruments may play the same part. Thus the chief function of the wind instruments is to provide a wide variety of tone colour, and (particularly the brass) a considerable range of power at points of climax.

The percussion is mainly concerned with reinforcing accents and rhythms. The harp is mostly used to add special colour, usually in the form of chords, *arpeggios* and *glissandos*.

——— The concert platform ———

The arrangement of the players on the concert platform varies, but a typical seating plan is shown opposite.

——— Additional instruments ———

From time to time composers call for additional wind instruments which are not normally included in orchestral scores. Examples of works in which these instruments are to be found are given on page 119.

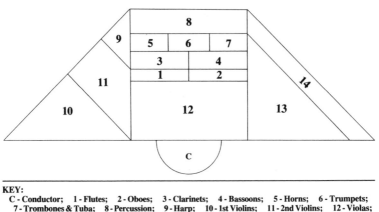

KEY:
C - Conductor;   1 - Flutes;   2 - Oboes;   3 - Clarinets;   4 - Bassoons;   5 - Horns;   6 - Trumpets;
7 - Trombones & Tuba;   8 - Percussion;   9 - Harp;   10 - 1st Violins;   11 - 2nd Violins;   12 - Violas;
13 - Cellos;   14 - Double Basses.

—— Natural horns and trumpets ——

Before the application of valves to horns and trumpets, the natural instruments were able to produce only the notes of the harmonic series in which they were crooked (see page 116), plus a few uncertain horn notes which could be obtained by inserting the hand into the bell of the instrument. Hence the early horns and trumpets were crooked in whichever key would enable the composer to make the best use of the limited series of notes.

The table which follows shows how natural horns and trumpets actually sound when crooked in various keys. When reading the full scores of the older composers, the appropriate transpositions have to be made, e.g. notes for the horn in D must be read a minor seventh lower than written.

Horn crooked in	*Sounds*
B flat alto	A tone lower than written
A	A minor third lower than written
A flat	A major third lower than written
G	A perfect fourth lower than written
F	A perfect fifth lower than written

E	A minor sixth lower than written
E flat	A major sixth lower than written
D	A minor seventh lower than written
C	An octave lower than written
B flat basso	A major ninth lower than written

Trumpet crooked in

F	A perfect fourth higher than written
E	A major third higher than written
E flat	A minor third higher than written
D	A major second higher than written
C	As written
B flat	A major second lower than written
A	A minor third lower than written

——— Smaller orchestras ———

'Orchestra' is an elastic term, covering almost any combination of players which includes stringed instruments, but excluding small chamber combinations such as the string quartet with its four solo players. In an orchestra there are normally several players to each string part, but there are small combinations of solo string and wind instruments (sometimes also percussion and harp) which are regarded as 'chamber orchestras', and lie on the border line between orchestral and chamber music. Britten used such orchestras in his 'chamber operas' *The Rape of Lucretia* (1946) and *Albert Herring* (1947), each of which is scored for twelve solo instrumentalists, with the recitatives (see Glossary) accompanied by a piano played by the conductor. Schoenberg's *Chamber Symphony* in E major (1906) for fifteen solo instruments is in a similar category.

——— String orchestras ———

On their own, the strings form a most effective orchestra, for which many small masterpieces have been written: Tchaikovsky, *Serenade*

(1880); Elgar, *Serenade* (1893) and *Introduction and Allegro* (1905); Vaughan Williams, *Fantasia on a Theme of Tallis* (1910), etc.

A well-balanced string orchestra might be as follows:

No. of players	1st Violins	2nd Violins	Violas	Cellos	Double Basses
16	6	4	3	2	1
23	8	6	4	3	2
33	10	8	6	5	4

—— Theatre and light orchestras ——

The combination of theatre and light orchestras has varied considerably over the years. By the late 19th century, orchestras accompanying operetta became more or less standardised, at least in the London theatres. Thus the Gilbert and Sullivan comic opera *The Gondoliers* (1889) was scored for 2 flutes, oboe, 2 clarinets, 2 bassoons, 2 horns, 2 cornets, 3 trombones, drums and strings – a total of some 30 players.

With the development of syncopated music and musical comedy, the theatre orchestra underwent many changes. Often a piano was introduced in order to maintain a reasonable balance, or because the orchestra had, in effect, been replaced by a dance band in which the woodwind players 'doubled' on saxophones when required.

More recent developments include the use of electric guitars, keyboards, synthesisers and other electronic instruments. Microphone techniques and amplifications have considerably affected the balance between voices and orchestra.

The term 'light music' is elastic enough to embrace almost any music which is easy to listen to, from Tchaikovsky's *Swan Lake* (1876) to a popular film or television theme tune.

Although *Swan Lake* was composed for full symphony orchestra, much light music has been written for small orchestras which often include a piano to provide middle harmonies or rhythmic patterns, when such instruments as violas, horns or percussion are not scored for. There is usually a special piano-conductor part which, in addition to a part for the piano, contains the melody ('cued' in small notes), so that it may also be used by the conductor when a full score is not available. In the orchestral parts, important passages in certain instruments may be cued in the parts of other instruments, so that if one instrument is missing the passage may be played by another.

—————— How to read a score ——————

If you examine a few full orchestral scores you will see that (in most scores) each pair of woodwind and brass instruments is written on the same stave, and that each of the principal groups of instruments (woodwind, brass and strings) is arranged as far as possible in order of pitch – flutes, for example, are placed above oboes because their overall compass is higher.

Space can be saved by writing pairs of wind instruments on the same stave. When the two instruments have independent parts, they are written on the same stave, with the tails of the notes for the 'first' instrument pointing upwards and those for the 'second' instrument downwards (see the oboe and clarinet staves in Example 114), or if complex they can be written on separate staves to avoid possible confusion. When additional wind instruments are added to the score the same principles apply. The piccolo part is written on a stave above the flutes, and the cor anglais, bass clarinet and double bassoon on staves below the oboes, clarinets and bassoons respectively. To make the score easier to read, bar-lines instead of being ruled continuously down the page have gaps between different groups of instruments (usually between woodwind, brass, percussion, harp and strings).

In some scores all the instruments are named on each page; in others they are named only on the first page, and thereafter, when certain instruments are not playing, these are sometimes left out to save space. So, on the same page, you may find two or more scores printed one above the other, often with each score separated from the next by the mark **‖**. When instruments are left out of a score, those that are included are arranged in the correct order (e.g. oboes, bassoons, horns, trombones, strings).

In different scores the names of the instruments may be printed either in German, Italian, French or English. A list of instruments and orchestral terms in these four languages can be found on pages 231–233.

Now let us examine a page of the orchestral score of *Capriccio Espagnole* by Rimsky-Korsakov (Russian composer, 1844–1908).

In Example 114 overleaf the top stave is played by the piccolo, the second stave by the two flutes, the third stave by the two oboes, and so on. The four horns occupy two staves (two horns on each stave). The timpani part is written on a five-line stave, because the two drums are tuned to notes of definite pitch. Parts for the other percussion instruments - triangle, castanets, side drum, cymbals and bass drum – are each on a single line to save space, as these instruments are of indefinite pitch.

The first and second trombones share a stave, and the third trombone and bass tuba share the stave below. The 'a2' on the flutes' stave means that both flutes are to play the same notes, in other words they are to play in unison. A similar direction appears on the first and second trombones' stave.

Clefs and transposing instruments

The term 'transposing' is applied to those instruments for which the written notation is higher or lower than the actual sounds. There are two reasons for this. Firstly, to avoid the continuous use of leger lines, which may be difficult to read, and laborious to write. Thus, music for the piccolo is written an octave below the actual sounds, and music for the double bass and the guitar an octave above. Secondly, to enable a performer to change from one instrument to another of the same family, but of a different size. A clarinettist in a modern symphony orchestra, for example, has two ordinary clarinets, one pitched in B flat and the other in A, and may also be asked to play a small clarinet in E flat and a large brass clarinet in B flat.

Since the fingering of all these instruments is much the same, the player when changing from one to another naturally prefers to play from the same notation. In order, therefore, to save the player the necessity of transposing his part, the composer makes the transposition for him. If the composer wants the actual sounds in Example 113 (a), he will write

Example 113

(a) Actual Sounds   (b) Bb Clarinet   (c) A Clarinet

Example 114

V. Fandango asturiano

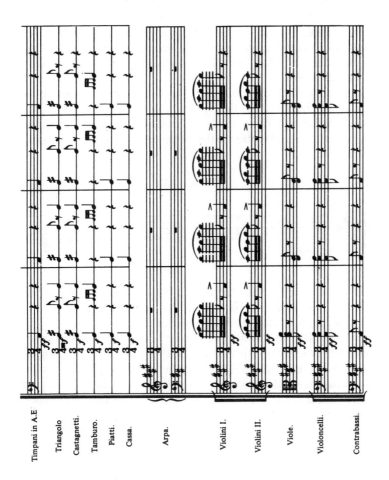

the notes a tone higher, (b), for the B flat clarinet, and a minor third higher, (c), for the A clarinet, using the appropriate key-signatures.

From the point of view of the score-reader, who is concerned with actual sounds, the position is the reverse of that of the composer; in Example 113, (b) must be read a tone lower, and (c) a minor third lower.

In Example 114 three different clefs are in use. The first and second trombones and the violas are given the alto clef, and all other instruments either the treble or bass clefs. Percussion instruments of indefinite pitch do not need clefs.

Until late in the 19th century the group of three trombones consisted of alto, tenor and bass, and the alto clef was usually adopted for the two upper trombones if they were written on the same stave. The part for the upper trombones, if written in the treble clef, would therefore sound as follows:

Example 115

In 20th century scores the group of three trombones usually consists of two tenors and one bass. If on the same stave, the two upper trombones are written in either the tenor or bass clef.

Most of the instruments in Example 114 have a key-signature of A major (three sharps). The clarinets in A have a different key-signature, because they are transposing instruments (see page 137). Looking at the first three bars of the score, the notes for the two clarinets are *written* a minor third higher than those for the two oboes, but the *actual sounds* are identical.

The horns in F and trumpets in A are also transposing instruments, but it has always been customary to write horn and trumpet parts without key-signatures, adding sharps and flats as required. Convention dies hard, and some modern composers still use this method, though others use key-signatures.

Although the piccolo and double bass are transposing instruments, the key-signature remains the same, since they sound, respectively, an octave higher or lower than the written notes.

Fig. 6
Sir Harrison Birtwistle (right) in rehearsal. The composer's music has highly original and often abrasive qualities.

The transposing instruments in Example 114 are therefore:

	Sounding
Piccolo	An octave higher than written
Clarinets in A	A minor third lower than written
Horns in F	A perfect fifth lower than written
Trumpets in A	A minor third lower than written
Double Basses	An octave lower than written

Score reading

The professional conductor is able to cast his eye down the entire page of an orchestral full score and to picture, in his 'inner ear', not only what each instrument is playing, but also the total effect. In a complex modern score this may involve taking in 25 or more staves at a single glance, a highly specialised skill which can be acquired only through long experience and practice. However, the ability to follow a miniature score of a classical work, while listening to the recorded music, can be acquired with practice and patience. The beginner should start with the string quartets of Haydn (1732–1809) and Mozart (1756–91), first listening to the music as a whole, without trying to follow the score too closely, then concentrating on the first violin part (usually the melody), then on the cello part (usually the bass), and finally on the inner parts (second violin and viola).

He can then proceed to the earlier symphonies of Mozart, in which the few transposing wind instruments have simple parts which are relatively easy to follow. After this he will be ready to attempt more difficult scores, such as the symphonies of Beethoven (1770–1827).

In Chapter 7 the compass, technique and capabilities of the different instruments are discussed. The actual sounds can be appreciated only by the ear, and fortunately recorded music exists which illustrates the sounds of the instruments of the orchestra. Particularly useful is Britten's *Young Person's Guide to the Orchestra* (1945), of which records and miniature scores are available.

There is a wide range of published miniature and study scores of orchestral, choral and operatic works (also chamber and piano music) and many public libraries have scores on loan.

9

MELODY AND HARMONY

Melody is a succession of sounds which vary in pitch, are part of a regular scale, and are arranged in various rhythms. A melody has an implied key-note, or tonic, upon which many melodies start and finish, and it is the ordered relationship between the tonic and the other notes that produces what is called *tonality*. Since harmony has an important influence on melody, and melodic passages are often based on the notes of a chord, it may be logical to consider the use of chords before discussing the construction of melodies.

Triads

The basis of the chord system is the *triad,* which consists of a basic note, called the *root,* and the two notes a third and a fifth above it.

There are four kinds of triads:

Major, which has a major third and a perfect fifth above the root.
Minor, which has a minor third and a perfect fifth above the root.
Diminished, which has a minor third and a diminished fifth above the root.

Augmented, which has a major third and an augmented fifth above the root.

Example 116

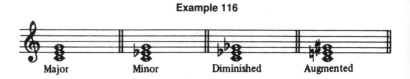

Major   **Minor**   **Diminished**   **Augmented**

Each kind of triad has a different character. The most usual triads, major and minor, are consonant and sound complete in themselves; the major triad is usually felt to be more cheerful than the minor. The diminished and augmented triads sound incomplete until resolved on a consonant triad.

A triad can be formed on each degree of a major scale:

Example 117

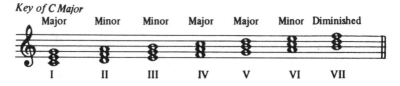

Key of C Major

Major   Minor   Minor   Major   Major   Minor   Diminished

I   II   III   IV   V   VI   VII

A triad can also be formed on each degree of a minor scale; the harmonic form is normally used for harmony.

Example 118

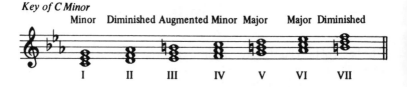

Key of C Minor

Minor   Diminished   Augmented   Minor   Major   Major   Diminished

I   II   III   IV   V   VI   VII

The three most important triads are those found on the tonic, subdominant and dominant degrees of the major and minor scales (i.e. I, IV and V). These are *primary* triads, whereas triads formed on other degrees of the scale are *secondary*.

Four-part chords

A four-part chord may be formed by doubling one note of a triad, in other words by writing one note twice, usually in different octaves.

Example 119

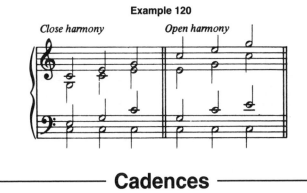

The best note to double in all chords is the root, though in a major chord the fifth may be doubled (but not normally the third), and in a minor chord either the third or the fifth may be doubled. The fifth may be omitted from a chord, but if the third is left out the character of the chord (i.e. major or minor) will be lost. Four-part harmony is normally arranged for four voices (soprano, alto, tenor and bass), two parts being written on each stave, with the tails of the notes going opposite ways, as in Example 120. The compass of the voices should be taken into account (see page 88). Four-part chords can be arranged in close harmony, with no interval of more than an octave between the upper notes, or in open harmony. Large intervals (e.g. octave or tenth) in open harmony are better between bass and tenor than between other parts.

Example 120

Cadences

A *cadence* is the name given to the melody notes (and their harmonies) at the end of a phrase or section of music. Cadences serve much the same purpose as punctuation marks in literature; some give the effect of finality, like the full stop, while others give a less conclusive effect, like the comma or semicolon.

From the primary triads three kinds of cadences can be formed:

1   The chord progression from dominant to tonic forms a *perfect cadence* (or *full close*) which, because of its conclusive effect, is nearly always used at the end of a piece of music. The two chords (V, I) are usually preceded by a different chord (often IV), which strengthens the effect of the cadence.

Example 121

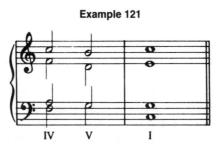

2   The dominant triad preceded by another chord (usually I or IV) forms an *imperfect cadence* (or *half close*), which gives the effect of temporary rest, and is frequently used to end a phrase other than the last of a piece.

Example 122

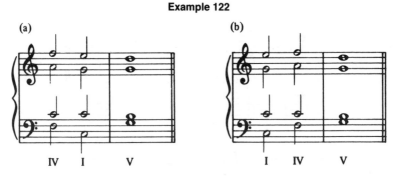

3   When I is preceded by IV, this is called a *plagal cadence*. It is also known as an *amen cadence*, since it is almost invariably used to harmonise the 'Amen' at the end of a hymn tune.

Example 123

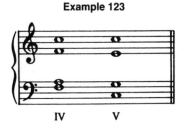

The effect of the plagal cadence is even more conclusive than that of the perfect cadence, and it is often used to extend a perfect cadence and strengthen its effect.

Example 124

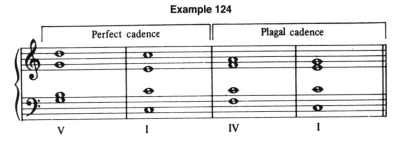

Harmonic progression

Different voices or parts of harmony move together in *harmonic progression*. Two or more parts moving in the same direction are in *similar motion*. Moving in opposite directions they are in *contrary motion*. When one part rises or falls while another part remains stationary this is called *oblique motion*.

Example 125

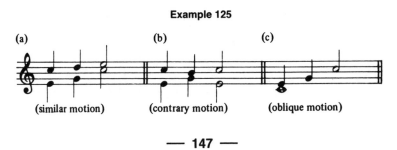

When three or four parts move together, two or three kinds of motion are often combined. When two chords are connected, the parts should flow smoothly, and each moving part should, where possible, go to the nearest note of the next chord. A note common to both chords should generally be kept in the same part, to act as a *binding note*.

Example 126

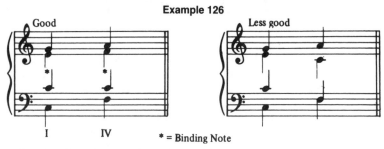

I   IV   * = Binding Note

Overlapping of parts should be avoided, except when a chord moves from one position to another.

Example 127

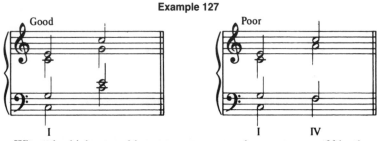

Good   Poor
I   I   IV

When the highest and lowest parts approach an octave or fifth, they should do so either by contrary motion, or with the highest part moving by step.

Example 128

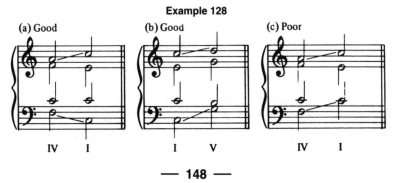

(a) Good   (b) Good   (c) Poor
IV   I   I   V   IV   I

The progression IV to V, and V to IV

The rules of formal harmonic progression (which should be observed in examination questions) forbid two *moving* parts to proceed in consecutive perfect fifths or octaves. The triads IV and V have no note in common, and when one is followed by the other, care must be taken to avoid consecutives. When IV is followed by V, or vice versa, at least two of the upper parts should move in contrary motion with the bass.

Example 129

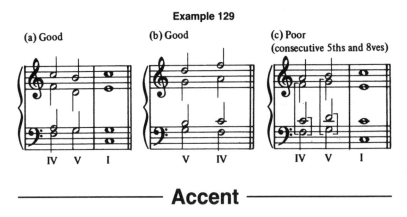

------------------ **Accent** ------------------

In a cadence which marks the end of a musical phrase, the first chord usually falls on a weak accent, and the second (cadence) chord on a strong accent. The cadence chord does sometimes fall on a weak accent, for example in the tango on the second beat of the bar.

In general it is better not to use the same chord from a weak to a strong

Example 130

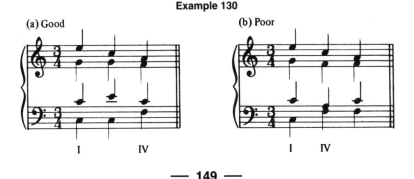

accent, and in triple time from one weak accent to another, unless it is also used on the preceding strong accent. The same chord may, however, be used from a strong to a weaker accent (see Example 130).

Inversions of triads

A triad which consists of a root with a third and a fifth above it, is said to be in *root position*. The root, however, need not always be in the bass; the three sounds can be *inverted*, by arranging them in a different order.

Example 131

Triad of C

(a) Root position   (b) First inversion   (c) Second inversion

In Example 131, (a) is in root position, with the root in the bass, (b) is a *first inversion*, with the root at the top, the fifth in the middle and the third in the bass, (c) is a *second inversion*, with the root in the middle, the fifth in the bass and the third at the top. The figures under the triads indicate the intervals from the lowest note of each chord. In practice, root position chords are not usually figured; and first inversion chords are figured 6 (and known as a 'chord of the sixth'), since it is assumed that each chord will contain a third. Alternatively, inversions can be referred to by their Roman numerals, with the addition of *b* (first inversion) and *c* (second inversion).

Example 132

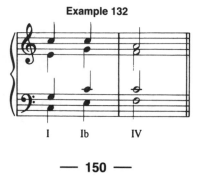

The judicious use of first inversions lends variety and flow to the harmony, and avoids the monotonous movement of the bass part. Primary triads in four-part harmony in first inversion usually sound better if the root or fifth is doubled, rather than the third.

When two first inversions (e.g. IVb and Vb) are used in succession, care must be taken to avoid consecutive fifths and octaves; if the top part moves in sixths with the bass, the root and fifth should be doubled alternately.

Example 133

The use of the second inversion is restricted – the most useful progression is Ic resolving on V – this often occurs at a cadence, and is known as a *cadential six-four*. The best note to double is the bass note; the other two notes usually move by step.

Example 134

(a)   (b)   (c)

   Ic   V   Ic   V   Ic   V

To obtain a smooth progression between Ic and V, the sixth and fourth (from the bass) of the first chord should fall to the fifth and third of the second chord, and Ic should not be placed on a weaker beat than V. When the outer parts of a second inversion are a perfect fourth apart, they should not be approached by similar motion.

Example 135

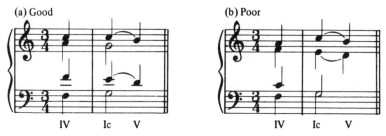

(a) Good   (b) Poor

     IV   Ic   V   IV   Ic   V

The passing six-four

Another use of the second inversion is as a decorative chord on a weak accent, between I and Ib, or IV and IVb; the bass then moves in contrary motion with the treble.

Example 136

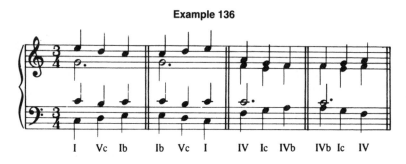

   I   Vc   Ib   Ib   Vc   I   IV   Ic   IVb   IVb   Ic   IV

—— Primary triads in the minor key ——

Of the triads formed on the degrees of the harmonic minor scale those on the tonic and subdominant are minor, but the dominant triad remains major because of the sharpened leading note.

In general, recommendations relating to primary triads in a major key apply equally to those in a minor key, and a progression in a major key may be turned into the key of its tonic minor by changing the key-signature and sharpening the leading note.

Example 137

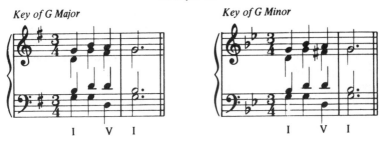

Key of G Major   *Key of G Minor*

The interval of an augmented second between the sixth and seventh degrees of the harmonic minor scale should be avoided. In moving from IV to V, therefore, the seventh degree should be approached from above.

Example 138

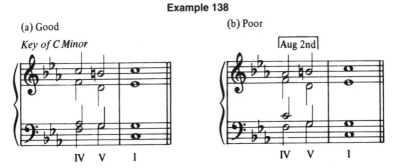

(a) Good   (b) Poor

Key of C Minor   Aug 2nd

When V is followed by IV, the seventh degree should rise to the octave, and the sixth should be approached from below.

Example 139

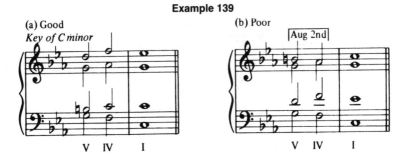

(a) Good   (b) Poor

Key of C minor   Aug 2nd

In the harmonic scale IVb cannot be followed by Vb, or vice versa, as the bass notes of the two chords would form an augmented second.* Other progressions which are satisfactory in the major key may also be used in the minor.

Sometimes the final chord of a piece in a minor key will contain a major third in place of the expected minor third. This chromatic note, which gives a greater sense of finality, is known as a *tierce de picardie* (i.e. Picardy third). It was in common use during the 16th century and Baroque period. †

Example 140

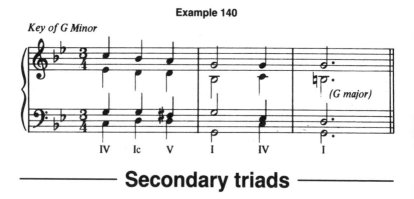

──────── Secondary triads ────────

Secondary triads occur on the second, third, sixth and seventh degrees of the major and minor scale. The primary triads form, so to speak, a

* This interval could be avoided by using notes of the melodic minor scale as in the example below, but care must be taken to ensure that the progression sounds smooth and natural.

† See footnote on page 179.

family circle into which the introduction of distant or near relations – the secondary triads – afford a welcome change. Two of the secondary triads are considered below and overleaf.

The supertonic triad

One of the most useful progressions is from the supertonic to the dominant; this forms a new kind of imperfect cadence, and a new approach to the perfect cadence, or to the cadential six-four.

Example 141

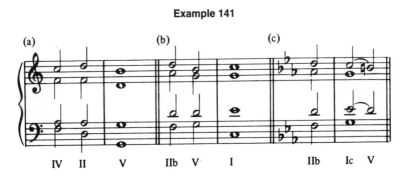

In major keys the supertonic triad is minor, and may be used in root position or first inversion. In minor keys it is diminished, and is usually satisfactory only in the first inversion.

The supertonic triad is effective when preceded by the subdominant triad, or by the submediant triad (see the following section).

Example 142

The submediant triad

This chord is most useful in root position, though the first inversion may sometimes be used.

When the dominant chord is followed by the submediant, a new kind of cadence is formed.

Example 143

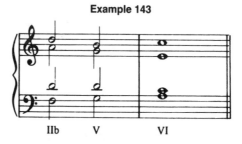

This cadence (V to VI) is known as an *interrupted* cadence, and gives the effect of rest without finality. In America it is called a *deceptive* cadence. There are other forms of the interrupted cadence, in which V is followed by a chord other than VI.

—— The dominant seventh chord ——

In addition to triads there are many chords which consist of four or more different notes. If we take a triad and add a note a seventh above the root we form a *chord of the seventh.* The most useful chord is that formed by adding a minor seventh above the dominant triad, thus forming a *dominant seventh* (figured V7).

Example 144

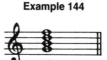

The three upper notes of this chord form a diminished triad, which sounds incomplete until it is resolved. The most satisfactory way is to let the leading note rise to the tonic, and the subdominant fall to the mediant. The fifth of the second chord is thus omitted.

Example 145

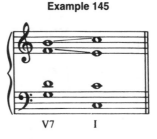

As the dominant seventh consists of four different notes, three inversions are possible (figured V7b, V7c and V7d) with, respectively, the third, fifth and seventh in the bass.

Example 146

The root position of the dominant seventh may be used instead of the dominant triad at a perfect cadence – the effect is equally conclusive.

Example 147

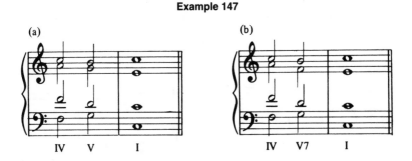

The inversions of the dominant seventh may be used freely during the course of a phrase.

Example 148

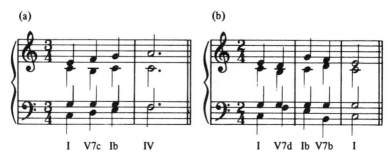

The dominant seventh may often be used with good effect on a half beat between V and I, between two harmony notes which are a third apart.

Example 149

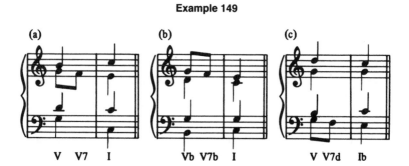

The inversions may also be used as inverted cadences.

Example 150

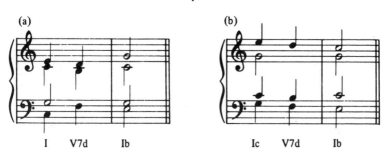

Example 150 (b) shows an inverted version of the cadential six-four. Inverted cadences preserve the flow of the music, by avoiding the constant use of perfect cadences in root position.

In the inversions of the dominant seventh all four notes should usually be present.

Example 151

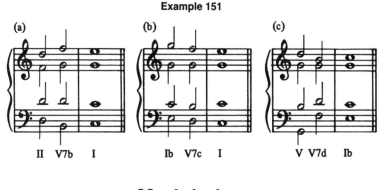

(a)			(b)			(c)		
II	V7b	I	Ib	V7c	I	V	V7d	Ib

Modulation

Music which remains in the same key throughout a movement tends to become monotonous, therefore it normally moves from one key to another during the course of the movement, and this is called *modulation*.

In this book only the mechanics of elementary modulation can be considered. When music changes key temporarily, the modulation is said to be *transient*, and is effected by the use of accidentals. When a key is established (sometimes with a new key-signature) the modulation is said to be *complete*.

In order to modulate from one key to another a chord must be introduced which is not in the original key (i.e. having one or more of its notes sharpened or flattened).

Though modulation to any key is possible, the simplest and most natural modulation occurs when the music passes from one key to another key to which it is closely related. The most closely related keys have the same key-signature, or a key-signature having one sharp more, or one flat fewer, than the original key-signature. Every major and minor key has five related keys: the relative minor (or major), the key of the dominant and its relative, and the key of the subdominant and its relative. Thus the key of C major has the following related keys:

C Major
A Minor

G Major	F Major
E Minor	D Minor

A modulation may proceed through a chord which belongs both to the old key and the new one; this is known as a *pivot chord*. If the new key has a key-signature of more sharps than the old one, the leading note of the new scale must be sharpened; if the new key-signature has more flats, the fourth note of the new scale must be flattened (or raised or lowered a semitone by the use of naturals).

Example 152

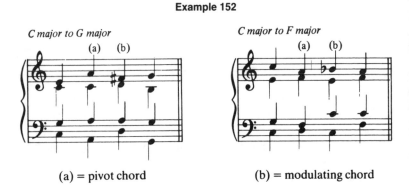

(a) = pivot chord   (b) = modulating chord

A modulation may also proceed through a chord which has one or more notes belonging to both keys; these are known as *pivot notes*.

Example 153

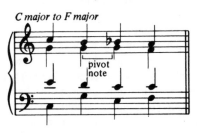

A series of transient modulations can be carried out by means of pivot notes, the dominant seventh chord of one key having a note in common with the tonic chord of the next key.

Example 154

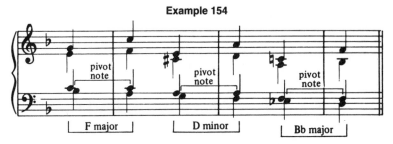

| F major | | D minor | | Bb major |

The tonic chord of the old key may generally be used to precede the dominant seventh of the new key, though other chords may be used so long as a pivot chord or note provides a connecting link.

Example 155

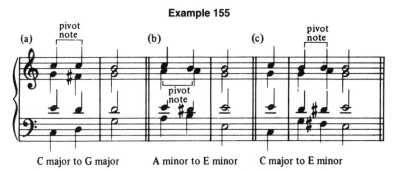

C major to G major   A minor to E minor   C major to E minor

Brief transient modulations, such as Example 155 (a) and (b), are often used during the course of a phrase, and give the effect of passing *through* a key. More gradual modulations (such as Example 155 (c)) give the effect of passing *to* a key, and are used when a modulation is to be established in an important position (e.g. at the end of a phrase).

——————— Melodic construction ———————

All music has some kind of shape and form.

Example 156

All Through the Night

Of the sixteen bars in Example 156 only eight are different, since the first four bars are repeated in bars five to eight, and again in bars thirteen to sixteen. This melody therefore consists of a musical thought (or *phrase*), a repetition of this phrase, a different contrasted phrase, and a re-statement of the first phrase. The form may therefore expressed as AABA.

In bars three and four, seven and eight, and fifteen and sixteen there is a falling off of melodic flow and movement; the last few notes of each of these phrases form a cadence. Cadences are classified according to the chords which are used to harmonise a melody (see page 145). When a melody is on its own, the chords are implied by the notes.

A melody, at its simplest, consists of a phrase, followed by an answering phrase of similar length.

Example 157

While Shepherds Watched Christmas carol

The melody in Example 157 may be expressed as AB, and is said to be in *binary form.** Each phrase begins with an anacrusis (see the footnote on page 25).

Phrases are usually of two or four bars, though other lengths (e.g. one or three bars) may be used. Also a phrase may sometimes be extended, or contracted, by prolonging or compressing a cadence.

A cadence which ends on a strong beat is said to have a *masculine ending*, and one which ends on a weak beat a *feminine ending*.

Example 158

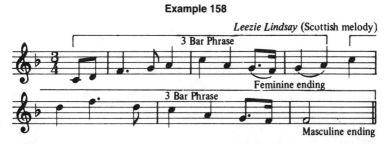

The recommendations which follow regarding melodic progression should generally be observed in formal writing, such as examination questions, though they are often ignored by modern composers.

A melody which moves by a succession of large leaps is usually ugly. As far as possible it should move either by step, from one degree of the scale to another, or by a leap of a consonant interval (see page 36). In general, the leap of a major seventh, all augmented intervals and all leaps beyond an octave, should be avoided, particularly in vocal music (intervals which are difficult for voices are often easy for instruments).

If a melody moves by a diminished interval, it should return to a note within that interval.

Example 159

* A melody which consists of a first section, a middle section of a different character, and a re-statement of the first section (i.e. ABA) is said to be in *ternary form*. A melody such as *All Through the Night*, in which the first phrase is repeated, is also usually said to be in ternary form.

Fig. 7
A section of the London Symphony Orchestra.

If a melody leaps by a sixth or octave, the notes preceding and following the leap should be within it.

Example 160

The leading note should usually rise to the octave, unless it is in the middle of a descending scale passage.

Example 161

The examination candidate is sometimes asked to add bars to a given fragment of a melody, so as to form a complete melody of twelve to sixteen bars, perhaps including a modulation to the dominant. Suppose that the given fragment is this four-bar phrase:

Example 162

The melody can continue with another four-bar phrase, similar to the first, but modulating to the dominant at bar eight. A contrasted four-bar phrase can then be added, followed by a final four-bar phrase which is a modified version of the given phrase, thus producing a well-balanced melody.

Example 163

Decorative notes

There are several kinds of decoration which can add grace and freedom to a melody. Decorative notes which belong to the harmony are called *essential* notes.

Example 164

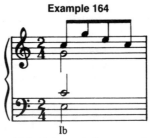

Ib

Decorative notes which do not belong to the harmony are called *unessential* notes, and include the following.

Passing notes

Notes that are used scalewise, upwards or downwards, between two harmony notes are called *passing notes*. If used after the beat they are *unaccented* and may occur in one part only, or in two parts simultaneously in contrary motion, as in Example 165 (a). If used on the beat they are *accented,* and are normally approached and quitted by step, resolving on a note which is not already in another part, as in Example 165 (b).

Example 165

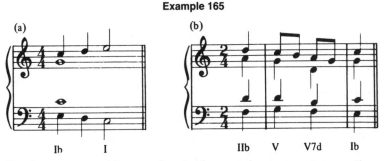

Passing notes normally move by step from one harmony note to another, up or down. Chromatic, as well as diatonic, passing notes may be used, but are rather difficult to handle.

The *appoggiatura,* much used in the 18th century, is similar in effect to an accented passing note, but may be approached by a leap.

Auxiliary and changing notes

An *auxiliary note* is a passing note which, after moving to the note a semitone or tone above or below a chord note, returns to the chord note from which it has passed, as in Example 166 (a) and (b).

Changing notes are used to decorate a single essential note, moving above and below the note, or vice versa, before returning to it, as in Example 166 (c).

Example 166

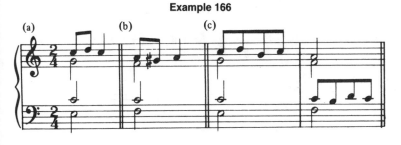

Anticipations and suspension

A note which moves to the note of the next chord before the rest of the chord is sounded is called an *anticipation* (see Example 167 (a)).

A note in a chord which would normally descend or ascend to the next note of the scale, but is held back until the rest of the chord is sounded, is called a *suspension* (see Example 167 (b)). A suspended note, which occurs on a strong accent, is resolved on a weak accent upwards or downwards by step (tone or semitone), and may either be tied to the previous note or sounded a second time. A suspension may appear in one or more parts. In Example 167 (c) the three upper parts are suspended over the bass.

Example 167

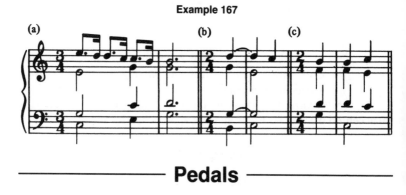

Pedals

A *pedal* (or *pedal-point*) is a note, usually in the bass but sometimes in an upper part, which is sustained or repeated through a succession of chords of which it may or may not be an essential part. The pedal should form part of the first and last chords over or under it.

Example 168

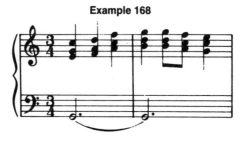

——— Harmonising a melody ———

We now have the following harmonic resources at our disposal:

Triads I II IV V VI

Dominant 7

With these chords it is possible to harmonise, in a reasonably effective way, most simple melodies (folk tunes, hymns, etc.). The procedure for adding harmony to a melody is broadly as follows:

1   Determine the key of the melody, and sing and phrase it. Then write under each note all the available chords in Roman numerals.
2   Determine the final cadence chords; if perfect, consider the cadential six-four; if plagal, use IV I.
3   If there is a modulation, plan the pivot chord or note.
4   Determine the other cadences, and then choose the remaining chords.
5   Write in the bass, trying to hear it with the melody; then fill in the chords, adding decorative notes where appropriate.
6   Check for faults (consecutive 5ths, 8ves, etc.).

An exercise in harmonisation will be found in the self-testing questions at the end of this chapter.

——————— Two-part writing ———————

The addition of a treble part above a given bass, or vice versa, can be attempted only when there is a basic understanding of elementary harmonic progression. Each part must be melodically interesting, and together they must form intervals which are acceptable to the ear. The intervals which will be most often used in two-part writing are the unison

Example 169

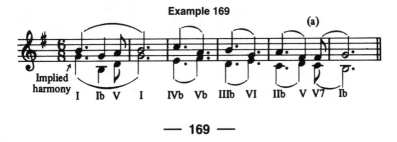

and octave, major and minor thirds and sixths, and the perfect fifth. The perfect fifth usually sounds better on a weak accent, unless it is approached by contrary motion.

The diminished fifth (or augmented fourth) sounds good if used as part of the dominant seventh chord, with the leading note rising to the tonic, and the dominant seventh falling to the mediant (Example 169 (a)). The octave is usually most effective when it occurs in the middle of three notes where the two parts are moving in contrary motion (Example 170 (a)), or when a note of the same chord has just occurred (Example 170 (b)), or when it is approached by contrary motion (Example 171, bar 3).

Example 170

The occasional use of unessential notes in either part will often add movement and interest. These are best managed when two melody notes are a third apart. The following may be useful:

1 Two notes a third apart: use passing note or chord note.
2 Same note in one part repeated: use auxiliary or chord note.
3 Two notes other than a third apart: use chord note.

Example 171

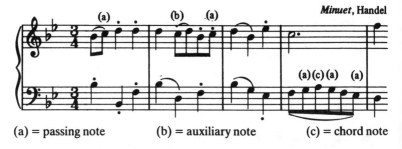

(a) = passing note   (b) = auxiliary note   (c) = chord note

Two-part writing can often be made more interesting by letting one part enter after another, with some kind of imitative device.

Example 172

When adding one part to another, first sing the given part and phrase it. Next, add Roman numerals to indicate chords which you think will make a good progression – there may be alternatives. Finally, add the upper or lower part, using contrary motion where suitable. Try to make each part melodically and rhythmically interesting, and look for opportunities to use some kind of imitation.

— Mediant and leading note triads —

The mediant triad needs some discrimination. Two useful progressions are firstly, when the roots of the mediant chord and the chord which follows it are a fourth apart, as in Example 173 (a), and, secondly, when the soprano part moves from tonic to dominant, as in Example 173 (b) (this is also good in the melodic minor scale, with the leading note unsharpened).

Example 173

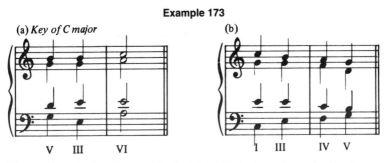

The triad on the leading note is diminished in both major and minor keys, and should be used only in the first inversion. It is often good where dominant harmony would otherwise be satisfactory. VIIb is actually an incomplete second inversion of the dominant seventh; it is usually best to double the third of the chord, and to follow with I, Ib or VI.

Example 174

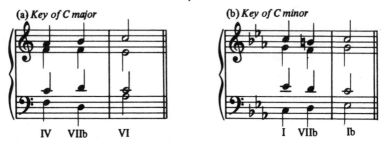

9a
SELF-TESTING QUESTIONS

1 Complete the following cadences in four-part harmony:

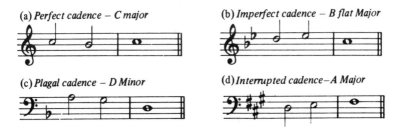

(a) *Perfect cadence – C major*

(b) *Imperfect cadence – B flat Major*

(c) *Plagal cadence – D Minor*

(d) *Interrupted cadence – A Major*

2 Harmonise the melody below in four parts.

modulate to
D major

3   Complete these bars in two parts.

Answers are on page 241.

10

EARLY MUSIC
(*c.* 1550–1750)

———————— Music before 1550 ————————

The origins of music are obscure. Pictures of early musical instruments are to be found in Egypt, China, Mesopotamia and elsewhere, and there are references to music in the Old Testament and in Greek literature, but most of the music that we can appreciate today dates back only to about 1550 AD. Before about 1000 AD, Western music was almost entirely melodic. In the early Christian church a style of chant known as *plainsong* was established by Pope Gregory I (*c.* 540–604 AD), whose name gives us *Gregorian Chant*.

The monks made use of modal scales (see page 33), and later began to experiment with *polyphony* (the combination of two melodies).* This was at first known as *organum* which, in its simplest form, consisted of the addition of a melody a perfect fourth or fifth below the original plainsong melody.

During the twelfth and thirteenth centuries a style of composition

---

* Polyphony has the same meaning as *counterpoint*, and is distinguished from *homophony*, which consists of melody with chordal accompaniment. The great master of counterpoint was Bach (1685–1750) whose contrapuntal parts have not only melodic and rhythmic independence, but also produce splendid harmony.

called *conductus* emerged, in which two or three parts moved more freely and independently than in organum. In the early thirteenth century the *motet* was introduced, and flourished throughout the century. The motet was a short piece for unaccompanied voices (usually in three parts), which was based on the lowest part (tenor), and was normally in plainsong form. [1]

In medieval times it was the practice to write plainsong melodies to some parts of the *Ordinary* of the *mass* – musical settings of the Ordinary as a whole were not common until after *c.* 1430. [2]

Music from *c.* 1550–1600

Between about 1550 and 1600, Italian and English composers were writing music which, though still based on the modal scales, was contrapuntal in texture, and abounded in imitative devices. The principal forms of sacred music were the mass and motet.

Secular music began to flourish, and the *madrigal*, a poem in several parts set to music, which was the secular counterpart of the motet, became popular.

Instrumental music also flourished, and simple keyboard instruments such as the spinet and virginals were to be found in the homes of the nobility, as well as chests of viols and recorders of different sizes. Italian *Fantasies* (Eng., *Fancys*), contrapuntal pieces in which the composer allowed his imagination full play, were written for consorts of viols, and suites of dance tunes and airs with variations were composed for keyboard instruments.

In Italy, **Palestrina** (*c.* 1525–94) was the greatest composer of this period. Most of his life was spent in Rome, and he wrote large numbers of masses and motets which display a serene technical mastery. **Andrea Gabrieli** (*c.* 1510–86), organist at St Mark's, Venice, was also famous as a composer of choral music with instruments, and organ music. His nephew **Giovanni Gabrieli** (*c.* 1555–1612) was also organist at St Mark's, Venice; as a composer he made full use of the *concertato* style, in

---

[1] From *c.* 1450 the motet became a setting of a sacred Latin text, for unaccompanied voices in two, three or four parts.

[2] The mass is the chief ritual of the Roman Catholic church; *see* glossary.

which a group of solo voices was contrasted with the full chorus, and also of purely instrumental interludes, or *sinfonias*.

From the Netherlands, **Lassus** (*c.* 1532–94) was the foremost representative of the polyphonic school. He travelled widely, worked in Rome and Munich, and wrote much choral music including masses, motets and madrigals. **Sweelinck** (1562–1621), a skilled harpsichordist, wrote keyboard and vocal music.

In England under the Tudors, music began to be highly cultivated as an art, and Queen Elizabeth I was generous in patronising composers of her time. To **Tallis** (*c.* 1505–85) and **Byrd** (1543–1623), who became joint organists of the Chapel Royal, she granted in 1575 sole rights to print music. Tallis and Byrd wrote some fine church music, as did **Tomkins** (1572–1656) and **Gibbons** (1583–1625), who were also organists of the Chapel Royal. Foremost among the madrigal writers were **Morley** (1557–*c.* 1602), **Bull** (1563–1628), **Wilbye** (1574–1638), and **Weelkes** (*c.* 1576–1623). **Farnaby** (*c.* 1566–1640) wrote keyboard music, and **Dowland** (1563–1626) songs with lute accompaniment.

— Music in the seventeenth century —

The seventeenth century was a century of musical experiment, and there were many new and far reaching developments. Among the most important were the birth of opera and oratorio, the beginnings of modern harmony, the establishment of the two modern modes, major and minor, and the gradual replacement of the viol family by the violin family, and of the spinet and virginals by the harpsichord.

The earliest true opera which was actually staged in Italy in 1597 was *Daphne* by **Peri** (1561–1633), a priest in the service of the Medici family. The story was told mostly in *recitative*, with simple *continuo* accompaniment (see page 69). As opera progressed, the *aria* was introduced, and this led to the conventionalisation of the Italian opera into a series of arias interspersed with recitatives. The first great operatic composer was **Monteverdi** (1567–1643) whose operas, such as *Orpheus* and *The Coronation of Poppea*, are full of music which is profoundly expressive and dramatic, with highly original harmonies and instrumental tone-colours. Monteverdi's pupil **Cavalli** (1602–76) carried on the operatic tradition of his master.

Towards the end of the century **Alessandro Scarlatti** (1660–1725),[1] a composer of over a hundred operas, developed the Italian form of overture.[2]

French opera, which was at first closely associated with ballet,[3] was developed by **Lulli** (1632–87) who had come from Italy to Paris at the age of eleven. Lulli established the form of the French overture, and employed *stromenta* recitative (with orchestral accompaniment) in place of the existing *secco* recitative (with figured bass accompaniment, played on a keyboard instrument).

Oratorio was first produced in the sixteenth century at St Philip Neri's Oratory in Rome, from which its name originated. The early oratorios were, in effect, sacred operas, and were performed with scenery, costumes and action; later, oratorio developed into a non-dramatic work for solo voices, chorus and orchestra, for performance in church or concert hall.

The rise of opera and oratorio encouraged the growth of instruments, and the improvement of their range and tonal quality. At Cremona in the north of Italy the great violin makers, Amati, Guarneri and Stradivari

---

[1] Scarlatti made much use of the *Neapolitan sixth* chord, formed on the flattened supertonic and used in its first inversion. This chord was popular for its pathetic effect with Neapolitan operas composers in the seventeenth century.

Key C major

Neapolitan   V
6th

[2] In the seventeenth century the French opera overture had a slow introduction in dotted rhythm, followed by a fast section in imitative style. The Italian opera overture had three movements – quick, slow, quick.

[3] Ballet, which originated in Italy and became established at French courts in the sixteenth century, is a dramatic entertainment performed to a musical accompaniment by dancers in costume. It was originally associated with opera, but later became an independent form.

produced their incomparable instruments, and **Corelli** (1653–1713), the first great violinist, composed violin sonatas, and established the form of the *concerto grosso*. This kind of concerto, which must be distinguished from later concertos for solo instruments and orchestra, has several movements, with passages for a small group of instruments (*concertino*), or the main body (*ripieno*, or *concerto grosso*), or both groups together (*tutti*). **Vivaldi** (1675–1741) was another Italian composer with a fertile imagination. His most successful works are his (older style) concertos, especially *The Four Seasons* for violin and orchestra.

A notable German composer of the period was **Schütz** (1585–1672) who, in his *Christmas Oratorio* and his three *Passions*, achieved a balance between the Lutheran polyphonic tradition and the Italian style.

In England, the most gifted composer of his time was **Purcell** (1659-95), who was organist of Westminster Abbey and of the Chapel Royal. Purcell wrote church music, the opera *Dido and Aeneas*, odes for royal occasions and for St Cecilia's Day, fantasies for strings, and much other instrumental music.

——— Music from *c.* 1700–50 ———

This is the age of Bach and Handel,* who were both born in 1685, but there were other composers of importance. In Italy, **Domenico Scarlatti** (1685–1757), son of Alessandro Scarlatti, was the greatest composer for harpsichord of his time. He wrote around 600 single-movement sonatas, mostly in binary form. In France, **Couperin** (1668–1733) wrote harpsichord suites (*ordres*) which are models of refinement and charm, and often bear fanciful titles. **Rameau** (1683–1764) was an important composer of opera, and the author of treatises which anticipated modern musical theory. In Germany, **Gluck** (1714–87) created a new style of Italian opera which replaced conventional virtuosity with simplicity and dramatic truth, and gave the orchestra a larger role.

* This period is often called 'baroque', a term borrowed from the lavish style of architecture during the seventeenth and early eighteenth centuries. The music of Monteverdi, Gabrieli, etc. is often called 'early baroque', and that of Bach, Handel, etc. 'late baroque'. Pre-baroque music is sometimes called 'renaissance', and late eighteenth century post-baroque 'rococo'.

J. S. Bach (1685–1750) was one of a large musical family. His second son, **C. P. E. Bach** (1714–88), wrote the famous treatise *Essay on the True Art of Playing Keyboard Instruments*, which is a valuable guide to the contemporary style of playing.

Bach was born at Eisenach, a small town in central Germany, and though he was widely known as the finest organist of his time, he received little recognition as a composer, living a quiet, uneventful life and, unlike his great contemporary Handel, travelling very little. He was a devout Lutheran, and this was one of the influences on his music, together with the contemporary styles of Italian and French instrumental music. He was a practical musician, writing organ and choral music for church services, instrumental music for his patrons, and keyboard music for his sons. His music combines masterful choral and contrapuntal writing with passionate expressiveness.

Bach's organ music includes choral preludes, toccatas and fugues (including the well-known *Toccata and Fugue in D Minor*). His choral music includes the *Church Cantatas*, of which some 200 have survived, which were composed for each Sunday of the church's year, the great *Mass in B Minor*, the *St Matthew* and *St John Passions* and the *Christmas Oratorio*.

His instrumental music includes the six *Brandenburg Concertos*, four orchestral suites (overtures), consisting mainly of dance movements, sonatas for solo cello and solo violin, and solo concertos, some of which are transcriptions of works by Vivaldi. Keyboard music includes *The Well-Tempered Clavier* (48 preludes and fugues in all major and minor keys), *Two- and Three-Part Inventions*, *Partitas* (suites), and the great contrapuntal work *The Art of Fugue*.

Handel (1685–1759) was born in Germany, and came to London in 1710, where his opera *Rinaldo* was produced. He became naturalised, and attempted to establish Italian opera in England, but when his fortunes declined he devoted his attention to oratorio. *Messiah*, his best-loved work, was performed first in Dublin in 1742, and then in London where the audience, following the example of George II, rose to its feet at the 'Hallelujah' chorus, a custom which has been observed ever since.

Handel's operas follow the traditional pattern of serious opera of the time: a French overture, recitative, arias, duets and choral ensembles. One of the female solo singers usually took a man's part (e.g. *Julius Caesar*) and two of the men were *castrati* (soprano or contralto voices produced by castration before puberty). His oratorios follow a similar pattern, but the chorus is used as a dramatic force, and to create grandiose effects. Handel also wrote church music and secular choral works, organ concertos, and *concerti grossi*. His orchestral music includes the popular *Water Music* and *Fireworks Music*.

Among the factors which contributed to the failure of Handel's operatic ventures was the production in 1728 of *The Beggar's Opera*. With a wittily satirical libretto by John Gay (1685–1732) aimed at the conventions of Italian opera, and sixty-nine favourite ballad-tunes arranged by Dr Pepusch (1667–1752), it took London by storm, and gave rise to a series of ballad-operas which temporarily eclipsed all other forms of stage production. A modern version called *The Threepenny Opera* by the German composer Kurt Weill (1900–50) was produced in Berlin in 1928 with enormous success.

11

CLASSICAL AND — ROMANTIC MUSIC — (*c.* 1750–1900)

It is convenient to divide styles of musical composition into periods, thus the classical period may be said to run from *c.* 1750–1825, and the romantic period from *c.* 1825–1900, though these periods are only approximate, and there is a good deal of overlapping. 'Classical' and 'romantic' are terms which should not be taken too literally – classical is often used to imply an acceptance of conceptions of form and structure, and romantic as being more concerned with emotional expression (classical is also sometimes used to distinguish 'serious' music from 'light' or 'popular' music).

—— Classical music (*c.* 1750–1825) ——

This period is also known as the Viennese School, since the principal composers of that time (Haydn, Mozart, Beethoven and Schubert) were all active in Vienna.

During the classical period less contrapuntal music was written, and many new and important forms evolved, in particular the sonata, string quartet, and the modern symphony and concerto. The foundations of the modern orchestra were also laid, with the harpsichord continuo giving way to the balanced proportions of the different orchestral groups. The overlapping romantic element is seen in the art-song (Ger. *Lied*) developed by Schubert, and the romantic operas of Weber – although both composers wrote most of their music before 1825, they more properly belong to the early romantics.

Haydn (Austrian, 1732–1809) became a choirboy in Vienna. He was the first composer to establish sonata form, and to bring to instrumental music the unity it lacked. His piano sonatas are usually in three movements, the first of which is in sonata form. He also established the string quartet, a combination which sounds complete without the support of continuo. Haydn wrote 83 string quartets and 104 symphonies. In his later symphonies he enlarged the orchestra to include flutes and clarinets, and in his *Military* symphony he added triangle, bass drum and cymbals to the usual timpani. He also wrote many piano sonatas, and two large choral works — *The Creation* and *The Seasons*.

Mozart (Austrian, 1756–91) became a child prodigy as a harpsichordist, travelling widely in Europe. At the age of 25 he settled in Vienna. Mozart composed in every form known in his time. Music flowed freely from his pen, and Haydn regarded him as the greatest composer of the age. He wrote 41 symphonies (including the popular E flat major, G minor, and C major (*Jupiter*)), many concertos for piano and other instruments, much chamber and piano music, and many operas (e.g. *The Marriage of Figaro*, *The Magic Flute*), also church music, including a *Requiem*.

Beethoven (German, 1770–1827) settled in Vienna where he became famous. His childhood was hard, he never married, and from 1819 until his death he was afflicted with total deafness. Beethoven's music is divided into three periods: in the first period the influence of Haydn and Mozart is clearly felt; the middle period, during which the *Appassionata* and *Moonlight* piano sonatas and symphonies two to eight were written, enabled him to develop his individuality to the full; during the last period, though withdrawn into himself, he produced some of his finest work which reached into the future, though it was misunderstood by his contemporaries.

Beethoven's compositions did not come easily, and he often revised the ideas that he had written in his 'notebooks'. He wrote nine symphonies (e.g. *Eroica*, *Pastoral*, *Choral*), five piano concertos (e.g.

Emperor) and a violin concerto. His piano music includes 32 sonatas, and 21 sets of variations. He wrote 16 string quartets, one opera *Fidelio*, two masses and the oratorio *Christ on the Mount of Olives*.

—— Romantic music (*c.* 1825–1900) ——

This period may be divided into two parts: the earlier romantics (*c.* 1825–50), and the later romantics (*c.* 1850–1900). The first part includes the operatic composers Weber, Meyerbeer, Rossini and Glinka; and Schubert, Berlioz, Mendelssohn, Chopin and Schumann. The second part includes the nationalist composers (e.g. Rimsky-Korsakov, Dvořák, Grieg), and many other important composers such as Liszt, Wagner, Verdi, Brahms and Tchaikovsky.

Early romantics (c. 1825–50)

Weber (German, 1786–1826) held many appointments as conductor in German opera houses. His piano sonatas, chamber and orchestral music, and concertos are mostly forgotten – his importance is as the creator of German romantic opera, especially *Der Freischütz* with its magic and supernatural elements. His other operas include *Oberon*, first performed in London at Covent Garden.

Towards the beginning of the nineteenth century the German-born **Meyerbeer** (1791–1864) went to Italy and composed operas in the Italian style. He later went to Paris where his spectacular and elaborate operas (e.g. *Robert le Diable*, *Les Huguenots*, *L'Africaine*) won acclaim. Wagner, though highly critical of Meyerbeer, was nevertheless influenced by his style, and his original and effective orchestration.

Rossini (1792–1868) was the greatest Italian operatic composer of his time, and a master of vocal melody and orchestration. The *Barber of Seville* and *William Tell* were the most successful of his 36 operas. He retired from operatic composition at the age of 37, though he later wrote his *Stabat Mater*.

Schubert (Austrian, 1797–1828) became a chorister at the Imperial Chapel in Vienna, and later the leader of the chapel orchestra. He was a prolific composer, and melody seemed to come naturally to him, but he failed to gain any musical position of importance, and died in poverty at the age of 31 of typhus.

Schubert's greatest contribution was as a writer of more than 600 songs, the style of which covers a wide range from utmost simplicity to intense drama, and the form and piano accompaniment seems to grow from the poetry of the words. Single songs include *The Erl King* and *Hark, Hark the Lark*. He also wrote the song cycles *The Maid of the Mill* and *Winter Journey*. Orchestral music includes nine symphonies (e. g. the *Tragic, Unfinished* and *Great*), and his chamber music includes *Death and the Maiden* string quartet with variations on the composer's song of that title, and the *Trout* quintet for strings and piano. There are also piano sonatas and choral works.

Berlioz (1803–69) was the son of a French doctor who sent him to Paris to study medicine. He later entered the Paris Conservatoire, and eventually won the *Prix de Rome* with an early cantata. Berlioz was a great orchestral innovator who founded (with Meyerbeer) the style of orchestration which we look upon as modern, and which was further developed by Wagner. Berlioz often wrote for huge orchestras, and published a valuable treatise on orchestration. His life was tempestuous – he fell in love and married Harriet Smithson, an Irish actress who inspired his *Fantastic Symphony*. They separated, and his last years were filled with disillusionment and depression. He wrote three operas (e. g. *The Trojans*), *Harold in Italy* for viola and orchestra, overtures (e. g. *Roman Carnival*), choral works including *Requiem Mass, L'Enfance du Christ* and *Te Deum*, and songs.

Glinka (1804–57) was the first important Russian operatic composer. He studied opera in Italy, and later in Berlin. He wrote two Russian operas: *A Life for the Czar* and *Russlan and Ludmilla*.

Mendelssohn (German, 1809–47) was the son of wealthy Jewish parents. He was a pianist, conductor and composer from an early age – he wrote his string octet at 16 and his *Midsummer Night's Dream* overture at 17. He visited England where he conducted the Philharmonic Society, and Scotland which inspired *The Hebrides* overture and *Scotch* symphony. His music, which displays considerable craftsmanship and contrapuntal skill, includes five symphonies (e. g. *Italian*), four overtures for concert performance, two concertos for piano and one for violin, oratorios (e. g. *Elijah, St Paul*), chamber, piano and organ music, and songs.

Chopin (Polish, 1810–49) was a musical prodigy, and developed a new style of piano playing and composition. He travelled widely, giving concert tours in Germany and England, and visiting Majorca with George Sand the novelist, who nursed him devotedly through the earlier stages of tuberculosis, from which he died at an early age. Chopin's music is almost entirely for the piano, for which he wrote mostly small-scale works: preludes (one in every major and minor key), *études*, nocturnes, waltzes, polonaises and mazurkas (the latter strongly influenced by Polish folk music). His larger works include ballades, scherzos, sonatas, and two concertos for piano and orchestra.

Schumann (German, 1810–56) gave up the study of law for music, but having injured his hand with a device he invented for developing his fingers, had to give up his career as a pianist for that of a composer. He married Clara Wieck who became famous as a pianist, and played many of his compositions. During his later years he was increasingly affected by mental instability, and he died in an asylum. Schumann's style was most successful in his piano writing, which combines rhythmic variety with richness and warmth. His orchestral writing is sometimes ineffective, and lacking a sense of colour. Schumann wrote four symphonies, and concertos for piano and for cello. His principal piano works include three sonatas, and many sets of pieces with titles (e. g. *Carnaval, Scenes from Childhood, Album for the Young, Albumblätter, Woodland Scenes*). He also wrote chamber music and a large number of songs and vocal pieces.

Late romantic music (c. 1850–1900)

Liszt (Hungarian, 1811–86) received piano lessons from his father and he became a brilliant concert pianist. He was also a great teacher and encouraged other composers, including Wagner who married Cosima, Liszt's daughter. Liszt lived in Rome after 1881, and became an Abbé. Liszt's piano music, some of which is of extreme difficulty, includes *Twelve Transcendental Studies, Twenty Hungarian Rhapsodies, Concert Studies*, and many transcriptions for piano of orchestral works, songs, etc. His orchestral music includes the *Faust* symphony, *Dante* symphony, two piano concertos, and twelve symphonic poems. Liszt applied these titles to orchestral pieces in one movement with a form more flexible than sonata form – he divided the 'poem' into different sections, and provided a 'programme' based on pictorial or literary ideas. * He also wrote choral music including the oratorio *Christus*.

Wagner (German, 1813–83) showed from an early age a great interest in drama and opera. His music, consisting almost entirely of operas, represents the ultimate expression of nineteenth century romanticism. He developed Gluck's reforms to their logical conclusion, writing his own libretti, fusing the literary, musical and visual elements into the unity of *music-drama*, and making use of the *leitmotiv* (a recurring theme symbolising a character, emotion, object or idea). His operas include *Rienzi*, *The Flying Dutchman*, *Tannhäuser*, *Lohengrin*, *The Ring* (a cycle of four music-dramas: *The Rhinegold*, *The Valkyrie*, *Siegfried* and *The Twilight of the Gods*), *Tristan and Isolde*, *The Mastersingers of Nuremberg*, and *Parsifal*. Most of his operas demand a large-scale production and a very large orchestra.

Verdi (Italian, 1813–1901) was mainly an operatic composer, but wrote a popular *Requiem*. In his operas Verdi maintained the Italian traditions of vocal virtuosity and tuneful melody, but gave them more genuine dramatic import. His earlier conventional operas, *Rigoletto*, *La Traviata* and *Il Trovatore*, were followed by works on a larger scale – *Aida*, *Otello* and *Falstaff* – the last two being composed by Verdi in his seventies.

Offenbach (German, 1819–80) was sent to Paris in early youth, where he became a cellist. He composed a large-scale opera – *The Tales of Hoffman* – and many operettas such as *La Belle Hélène* and *Orpheus in the Underworld*.

Franck (Belgian, 1822–90) settled in Paris. At first an organist and teacher, he later composed a symphony, *Symphonic Variations* for piano and orchestra, symphonic poems, piano, chamber and organ music, and oratorios including *Les Béatitudes*.

---

* *Programme music* is now applied to music whose form is related to a story or image and is therefore the opposite of *absolute music*, which is music which exists simply as such, without association outside itself. The symphonic poem was adopted by many nationalist composers (e. g. Smetana, *Má Vlast*; Borodin, *In the Steppes of Central Asia*; Sibelius, *Finlandia*). Programme music includes 'programme symphonies', such as Beethoven's *Pastoral* symphony, and Berlioz's *Fantastic Symphony*.

Smetana (1824–84), the first Czech composer of importance, wrote several operas on national subjects, including *The Bartered Bride*. He also wrote symphonic poems, the most popular of which is a set of six musical landscapes, *Má Vlast* (*My Country*).

Bruckner (Austrian, 1824–96) became a chorister, and later organist, at the Augustinian monastery of St Florian, but moved to Vienna to study musical theory and was appointed organist of Linz cathedral. During a visit to Munich he was greatly impressed by a performance of Wagner's *Tristan and Isolde*. Though he wrote no operas, his nine symphonies (one unfinished) show the influence of Wagner (he employed a quartet of Wagner tubas in three of his symphonies). He allowed well-meaning friends to cut his symphonies and alter his orchestration, so that the structure is sometimes impaired. He wrote masses and other choral works, as well as chamber, piano and organ music.

Johann Strauss the younger (1825–99) was born in Vienna. He toured widely with his own orchestra, and became known as 'The Waltz King'. He composed *The Blue Danube* and many other waltzes, polkas and galops as well as the successful operettas *Die Fledermaus* (*The Bat*) and *The Gypsy Baron*.

Borodin (Russian, 1833–87) was a chemist as well as a composer. His few works are full of rich, broad melody. They include the opera *Prince Igor* (completed by Rimsky-Korsakov and Glazunov (1865–1936)), three symphonies, and an orchestral symphonic poem *In the Steppes of Central Asia*.

Brahms (German, 1833–97) settled in Vienna where he held various musical posts. His music has both a romantic flavour and a classical austerity, and some of his works were influenced by Hungarian gypsy music and German folksong. He wrote four symphonies, two concertos for piano and one for violin, two concert overtures, *Variations on a Theme of Haydn* for orchestra, choral works including *A German Requiem*, about 230 songs, and much piano and chamber music.

Bizet (French, 1838–75) wrote his *Symphony in C* at the age of 17, and was later commissioned to compose incidental music for Daudet's play *L'Arlésienne*. He wrote several operas, including the popular *Carmen*, vocal music, and piano music, including *Jeux d'enfants*.

Mussorgsky (Russian, 1839–81) was intended for a military career, but resigned his commission to study music. His best-known works include the opera *Boris Godunov*, the piano solo *Pictures at an Exhibition* (later orchestrated by Ravel), and the orchestral tone poem *Night on the Bare Mountain*. He also wrote many songs, and was inspired by Russian folk music.

Tchaikovsky (Russian, 1840–93) started composing when he was 14. He was the first Russian composer to achieve recognition outside Russia, making international tours and visiting the USA and London. His music is full of rich, warm-hearted melodies, and his orchestration is colourful and brilliant. His compositions include six symphonies, piano concertos (the first is probably the most popular ever written), a violin concerto, operas (including *Eugene Onegin* and *The Queen of Spades*), ballets (including *Swan Lake*, *Sleeping Beauty* and *Nutcracker*), the overture-fantasia *Romeo and Juliet*, *Serenade in C* for string orchestra, and chamber, piano and vocal music.

Dvořák (Czech, 1841–1904) was at first a viola player, but encouraged by Brahms he was able to devote himself entirely to composition, and made visits to England, Germany and America. He wrote nine symphonies, of which the ninth (*From the New World*) is the most popular. His other orchestral works include *Symphonic Variations*, *Carnival* overture, and concertos for violin and for cello. He also wrote some attractive chamber music, and choral works including *Stabat Mater*, *Requiem Mass* and *The Spectre's Bride*.

Sullivan (English, 1842–1900) entered the Chapel Royal in 1854. He won a scholarship to study at the Leipzig Conservatoire, and later became organist at St Michael's, Chester Square. Although he composed much serious music, his fame rests with his Savoy Operas (with Gilbert as librettist), which include *The Pirates of Penzance*, *Iolanthe*, *The Mikado*, and *The Yeomen of the Guard*.

Grieg (Norwegian, 1843–1907) began composing when he was nine. After studying in Leipzig and Copenhagen, he became interested in the nationalist movement in music, and in his compositions he made frequent use of Norwegian traditional rhythms. He was most successful with the smaller musical forms, though his piano concerto remains one of the most popular works of its kind. He wrote incidental music for Ibsen's play *Peer Gynt*, the *Holberg Suite* for strings, piano music including ten books of *Lyric Pieces*, many songs, and some chamber music.

Rimsky-Korsakov (Russian, 1844–1908) became a naval officer before he devoted himself to music. He taught many young Russian composers (including Stravinsky), and wrote a treatise on orchestration illustrated entirely from his own works. He composed several operas, of which *The Golden Cockerel* was the most successful; also the symphonic suite *Schéhérazade*, three symphonies, and many songs.

12

THE MODERN AGE
(c. 1900–)

Some of the composers writing at the end of the 19th and the beginning of the 20th centuries further developed the romantic tradition. They include Elgar, Mahler, Richard Strauss and Sibelius. Other 'impressionist' composers, such as Debussy, Delius and Ravel, sought to suggest emotion by vague and abstract means, in much the same way that the impressionist painters reproduced in colour patches the effect of light upon objects, rather than the objects themselves in definite lines and surfaces. Often the appeal of music by Debussy or Delius is wholly sensuous, and the sounds of Ravel's orchestration wholly ravishing.

Other new groups arose, such as the 'neo-classicists', including Stravinsky, Hindemith and Poulenc, whose music was written for small rather than large combinations, and who made use of classical techniques such as the concerto grosso of Bach's time.

New systems of tonality and the dissolution of tonality were explored by most 20th century composers. Polytonality, the simultaneous use of two or more different keys, was used by Stravinsky (e.g. *The Rite of Spring*, 1913), Bartók and others. Atonality, in the sense of total absence of tonality and key, was developed by Schoenberg in his works from 1917 onwards, and by his distinguished pupils Berg and Webern. (This group of Austrian composers is sometimes called the Second Viennese School.)

Schoenberg became an 'anti-romantic' who postulated a twelve-note, or *dodecaphonic,* system which, though formed from the twelve notes of the chromatic scale, bears no relation to the classical diatonic and chromatic scales, since in Schoenberg's system the twelve notes of the 'row' are set out in a 'series', hence *serial music,* arranged by the composer. Although no two notes are the same, there are no 'degrees' of the scale, such as tonic and dominant. The sequence of notes is always used in the same order, but many variants are possible since the note-row can be used backwards (*retrograde*) or upside-down (*inverted*), and each variety can be transposed to any of the twelve semitones. Schoenberg also developed a style of half-sung, half-spoken declamation which he called *sprechgesang* (speech-song). He also replaced the homogeneous symphony orchestra with a smaller number of instruments, often with contrasted and unrelated textures, though in the final phase of his life he became more flexible.

Berg employed Schoenberg's basic technique with considerable flexibility, and Webern introduced new concepts of rhythm, texture and expression, mostly concentrated into works of very small dimensions. Serial compositional techniques (often combined with other new techniques) have also been used by composers such as Boulez, Stockhausen and Berio.

During the 20th century a number of composers have experimented with electronic devices. An early electronic instrument invented by Maurice Martenot in c. 1922 is the *Ondes Martenot,* which has infinitely variable pitch and variety of tone-colour. This purely melodic instrument makes use of *microtones* (i.e. intervals of less than a semitone) which are not possible on instruments such as the piano. It has been used by composers such as Messiaen, Honneger, Varèse, and by composers of film music. Another early system of organised sound was introduced by Pierre Schaeffer in Paris c. 1948, which was called *musique concréte* (Fr. concrete music); sounds recorded from different sources (everyday noises, percussion, voices, etc.) could be mixed, modified or distorted, and then assembled into a time structure. Pre-recorded sound has been combined with live performance, and synthesisers and computers of all kinds have been used for preparing, generating and modifying sounds. Composers who have employed electronic devices include Boulez, Berio, Stockhausen, Penderecki and Varèse.

A book of this size can only give brief details of those composers who may be considered important representatives of this period.

Saint-Saëns (French, 1835–1921) became organist at the Madeleine in Paris. His music, at first influenced by Liszt, includes the opera *Samson and Dalila*, symphonies, concertos for piano, symphonic poems (e.g. *Danse macabre*), the 'zoological fantasy' *Carnival of the Animals* for two pianos and chamber orchestra, and choral, chamber, piano and organ music.

Balakirev (1837–1910) was leader of the group of Russian composers known as 'The Five', or 'The Mighty Handful', which also included Borodin, Mussorgsky, Rimsky-Korsakov and Cui (1835–1918). He founded the Free School of Music in St Petersburg. His works include two symphonies, the overture *King Lear*, symphonic poems, songs, and piano pieces.

Fauré (French, 1845–1924) became organist at the Madeleine in Paris, and later director of the Paris Conservatoire. His style is essentially French, and his music includes the popular choral *Requiem*, *Pavane* for orchestra, incidental music for *Shylock*, piano and chamber music, and songs.

Elgar (English, 1857–1934) held some minor posts as organist and conductor. After failing to make a career in London, he settled in Malvern. His reputation as a composer was established by his *Enigma Variations* for orchestra, and his oratorio *The Dream of Gerontius*. Other popular works include two symphonies, concertos for violin and for cello, *Introduction and Allegro* and *Serenade* for strings, the concert overture *Cockaigne*, and the *Pomp and Circumstance* marches.

Puccini (Italian, 1858–1924) studied music at the Milan Conservatoire. Several of his operas have achieved enormous popularity. He was gifted with a vivid sense of melody, orchestral colour and dramatic effect. His operas include *La Bohème*, *Tosca*, *Madame Butterfly* and *Turandot* (completed by Alfano).

Mahler (Austrian, 1860–1911) born in Bohemia, held important conducting posts in Europe and America. Mahler's music was a link between the classic-romantic style and the music of the Second Viennese School. Several of his ten numbered symphonies, and *The Song of the Earth*, have parts for solo voices and choirs. His use of the voice and of the orchestra is highly individual. His songs include *Kindertotenlieder* for voice and orchestra.

Debussy (French, 1862–1918) is one of the most influential 20th century composers. His impressionist music employs many new concepts, such as the use of the whole-tone scale, and of shifting chromatic harmonies. His principal works include the opera *Pelléas et Mélisande*, the orchestral *Prélude à l'après-midi d'un faune* and *La Mer*, and many impressionistic piano pieces such as *Preludes, Children's Corner*, and *Suite bergamasque*.

Delius (English, 1862–1934) was of German parentage. Sir Thomas Beecham (1879–1961), the English conductor, was responsible for introducing Delius's music to Britain. His early works were influenced by Grieg, but his later works exhibit a highly individual melodic and harmonic style – to many listeners, much of his music has a 'wounding beauty'. His works include the opera *A Village Romeo and Juliet*, the choral *A Mass of Life*, concertos for violin, cello, and violin and cello, and orchestral works *Brigg Fair, On Hearing the First Cuckoo in Spring*, and *Summer Night on the River*. When, in his later years, Delius became blind and paralysed, his compositions were written down with the help of the English musician Eric Fenby (b. 1906).

Richard Strauss (German, 1864–1949) was the son of a horn player and became a successful orchestral and operatic conductor. He was a prolific composer, starting in his teens and continuing until he was over 70. His 17 operas include the at first controversial *Salome*, and the genial *Der Rosenkavalier*. He wrote several symphonic poems (which he called 'tone poems'), such as *Don Juan, Death and Transfiguration* and *Till Eulenspiegel*. He also wrote concertos for horn, oboe, and clarinet and bassoon, and many songs.

Sibelius (Finnish, 1865–1957) studied in Berlin and Vienna, and then returned to Finland. In 1897 he was given a state pension to enable him to devote himself to composition. His most important works are his seven symphonies, and his violin concerto; he also wrote symphonic poems based on Finnish legends, such as *The Swan of Tuonela* and *Finlandia*.

Satie (French (his mother was Scottish), 1866–1925) worked for a time as a café pianist. Some of Satie's techniques may have influenced his great friend Debussy, who orchestrated two of Satie's three popular *Gymnopedies*, originally written for piano solo. Satie's music is often humorous and satirical, with eccentric titles such as the piano duet *Three*

Pieces in the Form of a Pear. As well as piano music he wrote ballets, songs, and some longer works such as the symphonic drama *Socrate.*

Vaughan Williams (English, 1872–1958) studied at the Royal College of Music, and in Paris with Ravel. He became a teacher of composition at the RCM, and conductor of the Bach Choir, and was also an active collector of English folk songs. He wrote nine symphonies, including the *London* and the *Pastoral,* concertos, operas such as *Sir John in Love* and *Hugh the Drover,* choral works including *Serenade to Music,* and songs and film music.

Rachmaninov (Russian, 1873–1943) studied in St Petersburg and at the Moscow Conservatoire. He visited Germany and the USA, where he finally settled. He wrote three symphonies, four piano concertos (of which No. 2 is the most popular), and *Rhapsody on a Theme of Paganini* for piano and orchestra, as well as three operas, and piano music which includes a series of preludes.

Holst (English of Swedish descent, 1874–1934) played in various orchestras, and taught in colleges and schools in London. Like Vaughan Williams he had a great interest in English folk music. He wrote operas including *The Perfect Fool,* orchestral music such as *The Planets* and *St Paul's Suite,* and choral works including *The Hymn of Jesus.*

Schoenberg (Austrian Jewish, 1874–1951) was largely self-taught. His music became one of the landmarks of the 20th century. He began by writing music in the later romantic style, but soon abandoned tonality, and adopted his serial technique in its place, returning later to more traditional principles. In 1933, when the Nazis denounced his music as 'decadent', he settled in the USA. Schoenberg's music includes an unfinished opera *Moses and Aaron, Pierrot Lunaire* for *sprechgesang* (speech-song) and five instruments, a violin concerto, and much orchestral and chamber music. Berg and Webern were two of his distinguished pupils.

Ravel (French, 1875–1937) was a pupil of Fauré. His impressionist style is clear cut, and his orchestration masterly. His music includes the operas *L'Heure espagnole* and *L'Enfant et les sortilèges,* the ballet *Daphnis et Chloe,* orchestral works including *Rapsodie espagnole, La Valse* and *Bolero,* two piano concertos (one for left hand only), chamber and piano music, and songs.

Falla (Spanish, 1876–1946) lived in Paris for a while, and moved to South America during the Spanish Civil War. Falla was the foremost Spanish composer of his time, and much of his music was influenced by Spanish folk song. He wrote the opera *Life is Short,* the ballets *Love the Magician* and *The Three-cornered Hat, Nights in the Gardens of Spain* for piano and orchestra, and a harpsichord concerto.

Bartók (Hungarian, 1881–1945) collaborated with Kodály in the study of Hungarian folk music. Bartók's style is highly original and his music is often dissonant and atonal. His works include the opera *Bluebeard's Castle,* concertos for orchestra, for piano, and for violin, *Music for Strings, Percussion and Celesta,* the choral *Cantata profana,* and piano music including a graded collection of 153 short pieces called *Mikrokosmos.*

Kodály (Hungarian, 1882–1967) taught in Budapest at the Conservatory and University. His music, which is influenced by Hungarian folk melody, includes the opera *Háry János,* the choral *Psalmus Hungaricus,* concertos for orchestra, violin, and string quartet, and chamber music.

Stravinsky (Russian, 1882–1971) became the pupil of Rimsky-Korsakov. He met Diaghilev for whose company he wrote the ballets *The Firebird, Petrushka* and *The Rite of Spring* (the Paris première of this ballet, with its huge orchestra and primitive complex rhythms, created an uproar). Later he wrote works for smaller combinations, including *Symphonies for (23) Wind Instruments, The Soldier's Tale* (with speaking voice), and *Ebony Concerto* for dance band. Other works include the operas *Oedipus Rex* and *The Rake's Progress,* and the choral *Symphony of Psalms.*

Webern (Austrian, 1883–1945) began his career as a conductor, but later became a teacher and composer. His music uses Schoenberg's twelve-note technique in a highly individual way. Some of his compositions are of extreme brevity, and employ unusual combinations of instruments. His *Five Pieces for Orchestra,* for example, contain 76 bars in all, and the fourth movement lasts 19 seconds. His music includes two symphonies, *Variations* for orchestra, *Six Bagatelles* for string quartet, and some choral music and songs.

Berg (Austrian, 1885–1935) developed his atonal twelve-note system under the influence of his teacher Schoenberg. His principal works include the operas *Wozzeck* and *Lulu*, a popular violin concerto, and orchestral and chamber music.

Varèse (French, 1885–1965) first studied mathematics and natural history, but decided on a musical career despite his father's disapproval. He studied at the Paris Conservatoire, and conducted the Prague Philharmonic Orchestra before going into the army. When in 1916 his health failed, he emigrated to America, where he did much to further the cause of modern American music. He experimented with extremes of dissonance, and the sound ('density') of different instruments. His music includes *Density 21.5* for solo flute, *Déserts* for 14 wind, piano, 5 percussion and 2-track tape, and *Ionisation* for 13 percussion.

Prokofiev (Russian, 1891–1953) studied with Rimsky-Korsakov and others. He travelled widely, but finally returned to Russia. The astringent and discordant nature of his music became, after criticism from the Soviet authorities, more lyrical and popular in style. His music includes the operas *War and Peace* and *The Love of Three Oranges*, the ballet *Romeo and Juliet*, symphonies, concertos for piano, violin and cello, chamber and piano music, and *Peter and the Wolf* for speaker and orchestra.

Hindemith (German, 1895–1963) was at first a violinist and viola player. He composed for many kinds of musical media, and invented a new system of tonality which he expounded in his *Craft of Composition*. His large output includes the opera *Mathis der Mahler*, the ballet *Nobilissima Visione*, concertos, choral and chamber music, and songs.

Gershwin (American, 1898–1937) was trained as a classical musician, but soon began writing popular songs, and music for theatre and films. With his elder brother Ira as lyricist, Gershwin's song successes included *Fascinating Rhythm*, *I Got Rhythm*, and *Nice Work if You Can Get It*. In 1924, encouraged by Paul Whiteman the bandleader, Gershwin produced his first symphonic jazz concerto *Rhapsody in Blue*, which was followed by *Concerto in F* and *An American in Paris*. In 1935 he completed his masterpiece, the folk opera *Porgy and Bess*.

Poulenc (French, 1899–1963) was a pianist of distinction. As a composer his style combines clarity with satire and wit. His music includes the opera *The Carmelites*, the ballet *Les Biches*, concertos for one and two pianos, and for organ, strings and timpani, and the popular choral *Gloria*.

Copland (American, 1900–1990) was pianist, conductor and writer, and a stalwart champion of American music. His compositions, some of which contain jazz and Latin American elements, include three symphonies, *Statements* and *Connotations* for orchestra, concertos for piano and for clarinet, ballets including *Billy the Kid* and *Appalachian Spring*, and the opera *The Tender Land*.

Walton (English, 1902–83) was largely self-taught. *Façade*, an early work for reciter and six instruments, aroused much interest. His music includes two symphonies, concertos for violin, viola, and cello, the overture *Portsmouth Point*, the oratorio *Belshazzar's Feast*, the opera *Troilus and Cressida*, and the march *Crown Imperial*.

Tippett (English, b. 1905) studied at the Royal College of Music in London. The style of his music is often complex, and is partly influenced by the contrapuntal technique and cross rhythms of 16th century English music. His works include four symphonies, a piano concerto, *Concerto for Orchestra*, the operas *A Midsummer Marriage*, *King Priam* and *The Knot Garden*, and the oratorio *A Child of Our Time*.

Shostakovitch (Russian, 1906–75) composed his successful first symphony at the age of 19. He wrote fifteen symphonies, also violin, cello, and piano concertos, operas, ballets, chamber and film music. From time to time his music was denounced by the Soviet authorities, but though he admitted his 'errors' and undertook to find a style closer to 'folk art', he remained the most important Russian composer of his time.

Messiaen (French, b. 1908) is an organist, and one of the most original of modern composers. His music makes use of bird-song, plainsong, Indian music, and many other effects. As a life-long Catholic, much of his music shows his mystical devotion and religious ecstasy. In 1940, while imprisoned by the Nazis in a concentration camp, he wrote *Quartet for the End of Time*. His bird-song music includes *Oiseaux exotiques* for piano and wind instruments, and the vast *Catalogue d'oiseaux* for piano. Other works include the large-scale *Turangalîla Symphony* in ten movements, and *Transfiguration de Notre Seigneur Jésus Christ* for seven instrumental soloists, chorus and orchestra in fourteen movements. His organ music includes *La Nativité du Seigneur*, a set of nine meditations.

Cage (American, b. 1912) studied with Schoenberg and Varèse. The son of an inventor, he is also a pianist and writer. He invented the prepared piano, in which sounds are altered by placing objects on or between the strings, and for this piano he wrote a major work *Sonatas and Interludes*. He has explored aleatory music (in which chance or random choice plays a part), such as *Variations IV* for 'any number of people performing any actions'. His *4'33"* consists of complete silence.

Britten (English, 1913–76) started composing at the age of five, and became a talented pianist and conductor. The London production, at Sadlers Wells in 1945, of his opera *Peter Grimes* firmly established him and the tenor Peter Pears (1910–86) with whom, in 1948, he founded the first Aldeburgh Festival. Other successful operas include *The Rape of Lucretia, Albert Herring, Billy Budd,* and *The Turn of the Screw.* Britten's music, like Tippett's, reveals a deep compassion for humanity. His ability is most clearly felt in his vocal settings, where the influence of Purcell is evident. One of his most significant choral works is *War Requiem,* written for the consecration of Coventry Cathedral in 1962. His orchestral music includes *Sinfonia da Requiem* and the popular *Young Person's Guide to the Orchestra.* He also wrote chamber music, songs including *Serenade for Tenor, Horn and Strings,* and many folk-song arrangements. During the last years of his life he suffered a crippling heart condition. Six months before his death he was created a life peer.

Bernstein (American, 1918–90) was a man of extraordinary musical abilities. He was director of the New York Philharmonic Orchestra for eleven years, and was a prolific recording artist. As a composer he was equally at home with classical and popular music; he wrote three symphonies, choral and chamber music, and several musicals including the immensely successful *West Side Story.*

Ligeti (Hungarian, b. 1923) left Hungary to live in Austria and Germany. He is an important composer whose maturer works make use of 'advanced' idioms, such as the abandonment of clear-cut intervals and rhythms in favour of the colour, volume, density, etc. of the sounds themselves. He also uses electronically generated sounds. His music includes *Atmospheres* and *Lontano* for orchestra, *Lux Aeterna* for sixteen-part chorus, and *Artikulation* for four-track recorded tape.

Boulez (French, b. 1925) a distinguished conductor and pianist, first studied mathematics, then composition with Messiaen and others. In 1953 he helped to found the Domaine Musical in Paris, to promote the performance of new music. He was appointed conductor of the New York

Philharmonic and BBC Symphony orchestras. As a composer he is one of the most challenging figures in contemporary music, and his style has been influenced by the techniques of Schoenberg and Webern, and also of Messiaen and Debussy. He has extended the twelve-note technique to include new concepts of rhythm, dynamic level, articulation, etc. Boulez's works include *Polyphonie X* for eighteen instruments, *Pli selon pli* for soprano and orchestra, *Le Marteau sans maître* for voice and chamber orchestra, *Cummings ist der Dichter* for sixteen solo voices and instruments, and some piano music.

Berio (Italian, b. 1925) is also a conductor. Though he uses advanced techniques, including 'indeterminacy' (i.e. free choice for performance), his music is dramatic and colourful, and has gained considerable popularity. In his *Circles*, for soprano, harp and two percussion, he introduces spatial effects, in which notated pitches may be reduced to noise, and vice versa. Other works include *Allelujah*, a series of pieces for several instrumental bodies, and electronic music such as *Differences* for flute, clarinet, viola, cello, harp and tape.

Henze (German, b. 1926) began to compose at an early age and soon became recognised as an abundantly gifted composer with a wide range and variety of musical styles. During the Second World War he was conscripted by the German army, but after the war he established himself as a leading operatic composer with his *Boulevard Solitude* (1952), and later with *The Bassarids* (1965). He moved to Italy where he composed several symphonies, concertos and chamber works. His vocal music and many operas were much influenced by his preoccupation with the socialist revolution, and with Cuban politics.

Stockhausen (German, b. 1928) studied with Messiaen and became a leading exponent of electronic music. Later he explored indeterminacy, spatial effects, and fluctuating tempos, as in his *Zeitmasse* for five wind players, *Gruppen* for three orchestras and conductors, and *Carré* for four orchestras and four choruses.

Penderecki (Polish, b. 1933) is a composer who has taken advantage of advanced techniques, but whose music is not difficult to understand. His works such as *St Luke Passion* and *Threnody for the Victims of Hiroshima* have enjoyed considerable popularity. He has written a symphony, concertos for violin and for cello, and operas *The Devils of Loudon* and *Paradise Lost*.

Birtwistle (English, b. 1934) first trained as a clarinettist, and won a scholarship to the Royal Manchester College of Music, where with Peter Maxwell-Davies and other young musicians he formed the New Manchester Group for the performance of music of the Second Viennese School. His music, though at first influenced by Stravinsky and Varèse, and to some extent by medieval idioms, has highly original and often abrasive qualities. His works include the operas *Punch and Judy* and *Gawain*, *Trageodia* for chamber ensemble, *The Triumph of Time* for orchestra, and *Medusa* for instrumental ensemble and tape.

Maxwell Davies (English, b. 1934) won a scholarship to study with the Italian composer Goffredo Petrassi (b. 1904). After returning to England he taught music at Cirencester Grammar School, writing the carol sequence *O magnum mysterium* for the school choir, and later went to the USA to work with the composer Roger Sessions (b. 1896). He founded, with Birtwistle, the Pierrot Players (later reformed as the Fires of London), for which most of his works were written. His music is influenced by medieval devices, which he uses in a modern context in which original themes are parodied and distorted. His works include the operas *Taverner* and *The Martyrdom of St Magnus*, *Eight Songs for a Mad King* for voice and chamber orchestra, and much choral and instrumental music.

13

MUSIC OF THE PEOPLE

The beginnings

The beginnings of the people's music may be found in the traditional tunes by authors unknown and untaught, which were handed down orally by the peasantry from generation to generation, and often changed and improved (or corrupted) in the process. Many tunes have survived to the present day, and may be found in the folk music which exists in most parts of the world. Also in every age there have been classes of professional or cultivated musicians, such as the medieval minstrels who entertained feudal households, the troubadours and trouvères, aristocratic poet-musicians who sang their love-songs at the courts and noble houses in Southern France, and the German counterpart the Minnesingers. By the end of the 15th century guilds of minstrels had been established, and the craft of minstrelsy began to involve training in the reading of music, and in the playing of instruments. The higher ranks of minstrels were engaged to perform specific duties at court or in church, while the lower ranks had to pick up a living by playing at dances, funerals and other functions.

During the 16th century 'ballad sellers' sang and sold their popular ballads in the streets and at country fairs. Their 'broadsheets' covered a wide range of topics – historical, religious and political. The Puritan attitude to music and the theatre led to an increase of music-making in the home, and many collections of secular music were published, including rounds, catches, madrigals and dance tunes. After the Restoration, songs and instrumental items began to be included in stage plays, and were often collected in volumes. The public concert was also established in England by the violinist John Banister (*c.* 1625–79), and the coal merchant and music-lover Thomas Britton (1644–1714). The development of the concert continued, and by the early years of the 18th century formal concerts began to be presented, while smaller musical gatherings were held in taverns and coffee houses. In London, the Italian opera became a fashionable form of entertainment and 'promenade' concerts were held in the pleasure gardens of London (Vauxhall, Marylebone, Ranelagh), and there were musical performances at Sadlers Wells Music House. In 1724 the Three Choirs Festival was established, bringing together the cathedral choirs of Gloucester, Worcester and Hereford.

During the 18th century a considerable amount of music was published, including country dances, psalm tunes, operatic scores and incidental music, and since by 1800 the harpsichord had been almost superseded by the pianoforte, a good deal of piano music.

—— The Industrial Revolution ——

During the Industrial Revolution many working people began performing vocal and instrumental music among themselves, and in the industrial regions attempts to form wind bands led to the brass band movement of the mid-19th century. This became nation-wide largely as a result of the rapid growth of the railway system, and the invention of the piston principle as applied to brass instruments, the cornet in particular. The railways, and other steam machinery, were celebrated in industrial ballad songs, which sometimes voiced the protests and discontent of the workers. Before the advent of ocean-going steamers, there were also many 'sea shanties' which were intended to lighten the labour of hard seafaring activities.

The latter half of the 19th century saw the rise of the English music hall, which progressed from the public house to the theatre, where it flourished until the Second World War, and later found a new lease of life by moving back to the public house. Meanwhile, many now famous societies were founded, such as the Royal Philharmonic Society (1813), and the Bach Choir (1875–6). The Tonic Sol-Fa method of teaching music to choirs (using names for the degrees of the scale) became extremely popular, and was soon widely adopted by music teachers in elementary schools.

By the end of the 19th century the pianoforte, which by then was being produced in many shapes and sizes, was to be found in the homes of most of the more affluent classes. Many popular concerts were given in London at St James's Hall, the Royal Albert Hall, the new Queens Hall, and in other big cities, and concerts for working people were held at South Place Institute in London, where there was no admission charge.

English musical life in the decade or so before 1914 flourished as never before. Apart from the formation of the London Symphony Orchestra (1904), large concert orchestras were to be found at resorts such as Bath, Buxton, Southport and Llandudno, and a number of opera companies (such as the Carl Rosa, founded in 1873) were active. Large choral societies were established in many cities and towns, and the competitive festival movement was growing.

The USA

Popular music in the USA was at first made up of American lyrics set to imported tunes, although there were some war and political songs entirely of American origin. American popular music came under the influence of native songs and ballads, and of the folk-dance tradition (cowboy, Creole, French-Canadian, Hungarian, Spanish, etc.). Early forms of popular entertainment included travelling singers and 'singing families' from England (of which the Hutchinson family was the most celebrated), and 'minstrel shows' with their caricatures of Negro song and dance. One of the greatest early American composers of popular music was Stephen Foster (1826–64), whose sentimental ballad *The Old Folks at Home* achieved phenomenal success. The Civil War produced a spate of songs, such as *The Battle Hymn of the Republic* and *When Johnny Comes Marching Home*, and after the war the sentimental ballad flourished anew.

Social dancing

In the field of social dancing the waltz, despite initial opposition, achieved enormous popularity during the first half of the 19th century, fostered by the brilliant compositions of the Viennese Johann Strauss the elder (1804–49), Johann Strauss the younger (1825–99), and Joseph Lanner (1801–43). Other popular dances were the polka (which quickly spread over Europe, and became a craze as soon as it reached England), quadrille, lancers and galop. About the same time, a style of music called ragtime was becoming increasingly popular in America. This was probably inspired by the cakewalk, which is said to have originated in Florida. Both styles have syncopated melodies, straightforward accompaniments and a regular, march-style bass. Ragtime lasted until the end of the First World War, when it began to be overtaken by jazz, though ragtime has enjoyed a recent revival, particularly in the compositions of Scott Joplin (1868–1917), the black American pianist who was the acknowledged proponent of the 'classical' ragtime style – incisive bass, *arpeggiated* chords, and rapid treble passages. Joplin's most popular pieces include *Maple Leaf Rag* and *The Entertainer*.

From the early 1900s new dances began to be introduced to the ballroom, first in the USA and then in England, starting with the two-step, then the one-step (later known as the foxtrot) and then the Charleston, the Black Bottom and the quickstep. From Argentina came the tango, from Cuba the rumba, and from Brazil the samba, which became the basis of the bossa-nova. Around the 1960s, the Cuban cha cha cha had great vogue in the ballroom.

Many of the dance bands of the pre-war era, such as Ambrose (1897–1971), Ted Heath (1900–69), and Joe Loss (b. 1909), are now of great nostalgic interest, but during the 1960s, with the advent of the disc jockey and such programmes as 'Top of the Pops', live dance bands began to be replaced by the 'disco' of pop records played at a high dynamic level.

Jazz

It is probable that jazz originated in the negro quarters of New Orleans towards the beginning of the 20th century, and that it first attracted the

Fig. 8
Wynton Marsalis (centre) playing in New York, 1989.

attention of the English public when the 'Original Dixieland Jazz Band',
which had performed in Chicago as early as 1915, began a three months'
season at the Hammersmith Palais in London during the summer of 1919.
Traditional jazz, which is a style of performance rather than composition,
was originally played by small groups with one or more 'front' instru-

ments (e.g. trumpet, trombone, clarinet) and a backing of 'rhythm' instruments (e.g. piano, banjo, drums, string bass). During the 1920s alto and tenor saxophones were frequently added. One of the chief exponents of the New Orleans style of jazz was Louis Armstrong (1900–71), the black American trumpet player. The characteristic elements were spontaneous improvisation on old and new melodies, and pronounced syncopation in the melody, against a steady persistent rhythm in the bass.

The first decade of the 20th century saw the introduction of the 'blues', which began as a form of Afro-American folksong, and had much in common with the worksongs of the negro slaves in the Southern States of North America, though there was also the influence of the negro spiritual. Although there are 'happy' blues, the words are usually despondent and the tunes slow, with 'blue' notes (the flattened third and seventh degrees of the scale).

The 1930s saw the introduction of *swing* and the *big band* – the 12–15 players in the big band allowed powerful contrasts between reed (saxophone and clarinet) and brass sections. This was the era of outstanding soloists such as the pianist Fats Waller (1904–43), the trumpet and cornet virtuoso Bix Beiderbecke (1903–31), the clarinettist Benny Goodman (b. 1909), and of the band leaders Duke Ellington (1899–1974) a fine pianist, jazz composer and arranger, Tommy Dorsey (1905–56) a skilled trombonist and trumpet player, Glenn Miller (1904–44) trombonist and orchestrator who, before his death in a plane accident, led a famous service band, and Woody Herman (b. 1913), a notable swing band leader, whose big bands continued into the 1980s.

The 1940s brought a new style of jazz, using smaller combinations. It was known as *bop* (*bebop*, or *rebop*), and introduced complex rhythms and dissonant chords, against a background of a mainly improvised melody. Exponents of this style included Dizzy Gillespie (b. 1917) and Charlie Parker (1920–55). Other developments were *symphonic jazz*, played by large orchestras such as that assembled by Paul Whiteman (1890–1967) which used elements of jazz together with other resources, and *cool jazz* played by small combinations, with a gentle relaxed rhythm. There was also a trend which moved away from the rigid harmony of the bop era into a system of *modal jazz*, with solo themes improvised from the Gregorian modes (see page 175).

The 1950s and 1960s saw the development of *rhythm and blues*, a loud and lively variation of traditional blues.

Jazz-influenced idioms are to be found in the music of serious* European composers such as Stravinsky (*Ragtime for Eleven Instruments*, 1918), Milhaud (*La Création du Monde*, 1923), Gershwin (*Rhapsody in Blue*, 1924), and Copland (*Billy the Kid*, 1938).

———— Country and western ————

Country music, commercial music in American folk tune style, with simple rural lyrics, became popular in the Southern USA towards the end of the 19th century. At first it was known as *hillbilly music*, and often consisted of cowboy songs, accompanied by small string groups. From the 1930s these groups began to be enlarged into Western swing bands, which included rhythm instruments (piano, drums, etc.) and the electric guitar.

Country music became a profitable industry with international appeal with Nashville radio as its centre, and covered a wider range while mostly retaining its traditional style. One of the best known country singers was Johnny Cash (b. 1932) who made many 'protest' recordings such as *Johnny Cash in Folsom Prison*, but moved into gospel music (spirituals with a jazz rhythm) in the 1970s.

———— Rock and pop ————

A sudden departure from the style of the current popular music took place in 1955, when a recording by a 'country' musician, Bill Haley (b. 1925) with his group the Comets, of *Rock Around the Clock* was heard in the film *Blackboard Jungle*. Though seemingly new, this so-called *rock*

---

* What is 'serious' music? It is not easy to define, although musical compositions structured on classical forms (sonata, symphony, concerto, etc.) are obvious examples. There are many borderline cases, but perhaps 'music written for music's sake', as opposed to music directed to social or commercial purposes, might serve as a definition.

The terms 'popular' and 'light' present similar difficulties: a 'serious' work may be popular, and a 'classical' work 'light'. It is often a matter of personal opinion.

and roll was derived from a combination of rhythm and blues (black music) and country and western (white music). Rock comes in many forms, and the ingredients can include an improvisation over repeated two-bar phrases, with a harsh vocal line, lyrics which are often repetitive and sometimes sexually suggestive, laser and other lighting effects, and provocative gestures and behaviour. Loudness is an important feature of rock music; instruments used in rock bands include electric instruments (organ, guitar, piano, etc.) designed to be played through an amplifier and speakers, and acoustic instruments (flute, saxophone, percussion, etc.) which are amplified by means of microphones.

The most famous American exponent of rock and roll was Elvis Presley (1935–77), whose records such as *Jailhouse Rock* (1957) were great commercial successes. In Great Britain the Beatles, formed in 1962, became, right from their first record *Love Me Do*, enormously popular, and their record albums are known throughout the world. They were a group with charm, and the ability to produce excellent lyrics and tunes – John Lennon (1940–80), George Harrison (b. 1943), Paul McCartney (b. 1942),* and Ringo Star (b. 1940).

Another notable English group was formed in 1961 – the Rolling Stones, whose abrasive style began to rival that of the Beatles. Also about this time there was a revival of interest in the USA in folksongs; the most famous exponent of the new folk-music was Bob Dylan (b. 1941) from Minnesota. Dylan's recordings of traditional tunes, and his own compositions, combined country music and rock and roll styles, which came to be called *folk-rock*. He wrote many 'protest songs' about controversial issues such as civil rights and nuclear war.

Folk-rock was followed by the *West Coast sound* which used electronic feedback (instruments played in line with loudspeakers) to produce powerful screeching effects, and riffs (heavy repeated bass tunes).†

Another pop style of the mid-60s, performed by groups of black musicians, became known as *soul music*. It uses electric instruments,

---

* In 1991 Paul McCartney's *Liverpool Oratorio* (with composer Carl Davis as mentor and orchestrator) was given its first performance in Liverpool's Anglican cathedral.

† A form of rock music called *heavy metal* was developed in the 1960s by Jimi Hendrix (1942–70) and others, using strongly amplified guitar and bass, to produce a heavy volume of sound.

Fig. 9
Astro, singer, a member of the British reggae band UB 40.

and combines rhythm and blues with gospel music (American popular religious song), and other forms.

Many of the new styles are called *rock* (as opposed to rock and roll). They use, among other effects, pre-recorded tapes, synthesisers, and spectacular light shows.

In 1967 a Festival of Pop Music was held in Monterey on the West Coast of America. It was followed, in 1969, by an outdoor festival in Woodstock, New York, which was attended by half a million people. Later pop developments (1970s–80s) range from the melodious songs of singer–composers such as Carole King to the complex music of the so-called progressive groups such as Pink Floyd, Genesis and Yes, and to groups experimenting with electronic sounds, such as Soft Machine and Third Ear Band. The simplicity of the new wave of punk rock, which began its brief life in Britain in 1977 with such groups as the Sex Pistols and the Stranglers, influenced the music of groups like Blondie, Dollar and Human League.

Pop performers come and go, but those still popular in the early 1990s include the British rock band Status Quo who have had many Top Five albums, the Irish group U2 who have become one of the world's leading rock bands, British singer Rod Stewart who is still one of the big solo rock stars, American singers Michael Jackson whose album *Thriller* (1982) sold more than 30 million copies, Prince whose film and album *Purple Rain* (1984) made him into a top star, and Madonna, singer, dancer and actress, whose album *Like a Virgin* (1985) became a best seller.

———— Jamaican music ————

Jamaica, the third largest island in the Caribbean, was originally populated by Arawak Indians. Columbus landed there in 1494, and during the early 16th century it became a Spanish colony, and the first slaves were brought in from West Africa and the other West Indian islands. In 1655 Jamaica was captured by the English, and it remained under English rule until it achieved independence in 1962. Jamaican folk music has therefore several influences; Arawak, Spanish, African and British.

Worksongs are still performed by groups of folk singers. These songs, many of which have religious overtones, were composed and sung by slaves (who were not allowed to talk) as they were digging in the fields, or loading the banana boats. The singing was usually led by a *singer man* who improvised topical lyrics suited to the work in hand.

Music plays an important part in Jamaican religious cults, such as the Kumina groups and the Rastafarians, whose songs are accompanied by drums of various shapes and sizes. The most popular traditional song and dance is the *mento*, which resembles the Cuban *rumba* (though slower), and is accompanied by drums, maracas, etc.

During the 1960s a style of music originated in Jamaica known as *reggae* which subsequently became popular in Western countries. Reggae is derived from earlier Jamaican styles of popular music, including *ska* (influenced by rhythm and blues and mento styles), and *rock steady*, a slower version of ska. Reggae, which is performed by a group playing electric guitars, organ, percussion, etc., consists of a short bass tune (*riff*), the melody itself, and two contrasted rhythmic accompaniments. The lyrics are serious, and often depict social discontent. Notable Jamaican performers include Bob Marley (1945–81) who achieved international fame as a reggae singer and composer, and, towards the end of his life, incorporated African musical elements in his albums; and Peter Tosh (1944–87) who, with Marley, founded the influential reggae group the *Wailers*. Tosh, after leaving the group in 1974, produced a number of controversial solo albums; he was murdered by gangsters in 1987. In Jamaica live reggae has largely given way to the sentimental 'lovers' rock', and to the 'dub deejays' (disc jockeys) who recite over recorded music.

—— Calypso and the steel band ——

Trinidad, the most southerly of the islands in the Caribbean, also has a history of Spanish and British rule, before it became independent in 1962. Trinidad's two-day Carnival in Port of Spain is a national celebration, in song and dance, of the West Indian way of life.

Calypso, the best-known native music of Trinidad and Tobago, originated in the 18th century, when songs with witty, topical or satirical words were sung by slaves working in the plantations, with a simple accompaniment (e.g. bottle and spoon). In the early 1930s calypso became popular in the USA, and was developed into a commercial popular song with a distinctive Spanish-sounding rhythm, which was sometimes played by conventional dance bands. In Trinidad and Tobago, however, the calypso is usually accompanied by a steel band. Virtuoso calypso performers are popular at clubs and hotels, where they often improvise a song text about one of the guests in the audience.

The steel band, which was developed in the Caribbean during the 1930s, was originally an ensemble consisting of a number of oil drums with indented heads. Each head, when struck in different places, produced several different notes. Skilfully made *pans* have replaced the oil drums, with the band often consisting of ten or more pans. Although these are not standardised, the Trinidadian names for the three basic sizes are tenor pans (formerly ping-pongs), which play the melody, rhythm pans (including guitar and cello pans), which play the harmony, and bass pans, which play the low notes. Steel band groups are often accompanied by percussion instruments such as side drums, vibraphones, bongos, etc. The steel band has become popular in Western countries, and groups have been formed in many schools.

Indian music

India has a rich heritage of traditional music. The 'classical' period dates back to the 2nd century AD, when elaborate systems of five-, six-, and seven-note scales, called *rǎgas*, began to be evolved. There are now about 250 *rǎgas* in Indian music. During the medieval and modern periods, varied systems of basic scales, rhythms and forms were adopted in North and South India.

In recent years Indian music festivals have become popular in Western countries, encouraged by musicians such as Sir Yehudi Menuhin, the violinist and conductor. Indian concerts are often given by small ensembles of musicians, their length depending on the mood of the soloist, whose improvisation is governed by the strict rules of the systems. The main element of the ensembles, which vary from North to South, are:

1   Soloist (vocalist, *sitar*, violin, flute, etc.).
2   Accompanying instruments (a pair of small drums played with the fingers, called *tabla*, a folk double drum, etc.) playing a *tala*, or basic rhythm.

3   *Drone*, played by the *tambura*, a long-necked stringed instrument, or the harmonium, and usually consisting of the first and fourth (or fifth) notes of the scale played continuously.
4   Improvisation, according to the rules, since Indian music is not written down.

The *sitar*, the most popular instrument of North India, is a long-necked lute with movable frets, and five playing strings below which are twelve or more *sympathetic* strings which vibrate when the main strings are sounded. The *sitar* is similar to a much older instrument from South India, called the *vina*. The famous *sitar* player Ravi Shankar (b. 1919) has made frequent visits to London and other Western cities.

In modern India, film music, which is by far the favourite kind of popular music, is a blend of Eastern and Western styles and is often played by a combination of Eastern and Western instruments. Indian film music features prominently in broadcast programmes, and on records and cassettes.

Gamelan music

Gamelan is a generic term for an Indonesian orchestra. Gamelan music was originally played at the courts of Javanese and Balinese rulers, to accompany ritual dances and shadow plays, and for festivals and processions. It can be traced back to the early part of the first century.

Gamelan ensembles, sometimes with dancers, are becoming familiar in Western Europe and the USA, through concert visits (gamelan orchestras have twice appeared at the London Promenade Concerts). Gamelan music is based on a single five-note scale, but the rhythm is very complex, and there are twelve different varieties of phrase structure. There are many kinds of gamelan ensembles, both Javanese and Balinese. The instruments may include tuned single gongs, gong-chimes, drums, xylophone, bowed and plucked stringed instruments, etc. Several composers, such as Ravel, Messiaen, Britten and Tippett, have been influenced by gamelan music, and some have written new gamelan works (e.g. Lou Harrison, American, b. 1917, and Ton de Leeuw, Dutch, b. 1926).

African music

African music may be broadly divided into the music of North Africa, which belongs culturally to the Arab world with its long tradition of folk and religious music, and sub-Saharan music, the music of 'Black Africa', which has no traditional theory or notation.

Music and dance have a place in nearly all rituals and social activities of black African tribal life (work, ceremony, worship, entertainments, etc.). An outstanding feature of much African music is the complexity of the rhythms and polyrhythms (see page 226) resulting from unequal beats which do not coincide, often known as 'hot rhythms'. Hence the importance of percussion instruments – drums of all kinds, xylophones, rattles, gongs, etc.

The exposure of Africans to foreign cultures resulted in such cross-fertilisations as Afro-American music, which started towards the end of the 19th century with the importation of ragtime and black minstrel shows, and Afro-Caribbean music, which by 1940 had spread throughout most of Africa. About this time the introduction of the electric guitar heralded one of the most significant developments in African popular music.

Afro-rock, which was developed in England by Nigerian musicians in the 1970s, is a style of rock music with African characteristics which is often known as *highlife* and *juju* music. One of the most dynamic and provocative African musicians who found international fame in the 1970s is Fela Kupi (b. 1938 in Nigeria). He studied music in London, and returned to Nigeria to form a group and to develop his Afro-beat style, which replaced the dominant rhythm and blues forms with African rhythms.

Greek music

Greece has some of the richest, most diverse, and most distinctive traditional music of any European country. The Greek urban popular music which began in the early part of the 20th century is called *rebetika*. At first associated with an urban subculture of vagrants, criminals and hashish addicts, rebetika music consisted of songs sung in taverns, cafes and prisons, the words of which reflected the problems and feelings of their authors. Rebetika songs were often accompanied by the *bouzouki*, a metal strung long-necked lute played with a plectrum, or sometimes by an ensemble which might include a violin, accordion and guitar.

After the Second World War the bouzouki gained wide acceptance as the popular instrument in cafes and night clubs, with the music often accompanied by the ritual smashing of plates and glasses. Greek composers who have used rebetika melodies and rhythms in their music include Mikis Theodorakis (b. 1925) whose many songs and dances are mostly in the spirit of Greek folk music, and whose film score for *Zorba the Greek* (1964) brought him international acclaim; and Manos Hadjidakis (b. 1915) whose film score for *Never on Sunday* (1960) won him an Academy award.

10a–13a

SELF-TESTING QUESTIONS

1 By whom was plainsong established, and by what other name is it known?

2 Which seventeenth–eighteenth century composer was born in Italy, wrote over 100 operas, and made much use of the Neapolitan Sixth?

3 Which two important German composers were born in 1685?

4 Who wrote:
   (a) The Brandenburg Concertos
   (b) The Creation
   (c) Fidelio
   (d) Album for the Young
   (e) The Trojans
   (f) Finlandia
   (g) Il Trovatore
   (h) Tristan and Isolde
   (i) The Blue Danube
   (j) Pictures at an Exhibition
   (k) Iolanthe
   (l) The Rite of Spring
   (m) Pelléas et Mélisande
   (n) Salome
   (o) Serenade to Music
   (p) Pierrot Lunaire
   (q) Peter and the Wolf
   (r) Bolero
   (s) Bluebeard's Castle
   (t) Belshazzar's Feast
   (u) Peter Grimes
   (v) Threnody for the Victims of Hiroshima

5 Where and when did jazz probably originate?

Answers can be found on page 242.

GLOSSARY OF MUSICAL TERMS

—————— Abbreviations ——————

(The meaning of each word may be found by referring to that word under the heading Musical Terms opposite.)

Accel	Accelerando	*Leg*	Legato
Ad lib	Ad libitum	*Legg*	Leggiero
All' 8	All' ottava	*LH*	Left hand
CD	Colla destra	*Marc*	Marcato
Coll' 8	Coll' ottava	*mf*	Mezzo-forte
Con espress	Con espressione	*Mod*	Moderato
Cres; cresc	Crescendo	*Mor*	Morendo
CS	Colla sinistra	*mp*	Mezzo-piano
DC	Da capo	*p*	Piano
Decres; decresc	Decrescendo	*Ped*	Pedal
Dim; dimin	Diminuendo	*pp*	Pianissimo
DS	Dal segno	*Rall*	Rallentando
Espress	Espressivo	*rf; rfz; rinf*	Rinforzando
f	Forte	*RH*	Right hand
ff	Fortissimo	*Rit; riten*	Ritenuto
fp	Forte-piano	*Ritard*	Ritardando
fz	Forzato; forzando	*sf; sfz*	Sforzando; sforzato

Smorz	Smorzando	*Stacc*	Staccato
Sost; sosten	Sostenuto	*Ten*	Tenuto
SP	Senza pedale	*VS*	Volto subito

——————— **Musical terms** ———————

Fr = French; Ger = German; It = Italian; Lat = Latin; Eng = English

Aber (Ger)	But
Accelerando (It)	Quickening (the tempo)
Adagietto (It)	Slightly quicker than *adagio*
Adagio (It)	At a leisurely pace
Ad libitum (Lat)	As the performer pleases
Affettuoso (It)	Tenderly
Affrettando (It)	Hurrying
Agitato (It)	Agitated
Al fine (It)	To the end
All' ottava (It)	An octave higher or lower
Alla (It)	In the style of
Allargando (It)	Broadening
Allegretto (It)	Rather fast, but not as fast as *allegro*
Allegro (It)	Lively
Allemande (Fr)	A dance of German origin, usually in moderate $\frac{4}{4}$ time, beginning on the last semiquaver of the bar
Amabile (It)	Sweet, agreeable
Amore (It)	Love
Amoroso (It)	Lovingly
Andante (It)	At a moderate, walking pace
Andantino (It)	Usually quicker than *andante*, but sometimes slower
Anima (It)	Spirit
Animato (It), Animé (Fr)	Lively
Appassionato (It)	With much feeling
Aria (It)	A song with accompaniment, often in ternary form, known as *da capa aria*
Assai (It)	Very
A tempo (It)	In time (after *rall* or *accel*)
Attacca (It)	Go on, attack
Avec (Fr)	With

Bagatelle (It)	A trifle
Ben marcato (It)	Well marked
Bewegh (Ger)	With movement
Berceuse (It)	Lullaby
Bis (Fr)	Twice
Bolero	A Spanish dance in moderate $\frac{3}{4}$ time with the rhythm

Bourrée (Fr)	A French dance in brisk $\frac{2}{2}$ time, starting on the last quarter of the bar
Bravura (It)	With spirit, dash
Breit (Ger)	Broad
Brillante (It)	Brilliant
Cadenza (It)	*See* concerto
Calando (It)	Decreasing in volume or speed, or both
Canon	A polyphonic composition in which one part is imitated, after a short rest, by one or more other parts. A canon usually ends with a short coda, to bring it to a satisfactory end. Perpetual canons, or *rounds*, have no definite ending (e.g. *Three Blind Mice*)
Cantabile (It)	In a singing style
Cédez (Fr)	*lit.* 'give way' – slacken the speed
Chamber music	Originally, music suitable for performance in the room of a house, rather than in a church or theatre. The term is now generally used to denote instrumental music with one player to each part (e.g. string quartet), though 'chamber' may also be applied to other combinations (e.g. chamber orchestra, chamber choir, chamber opera)
Chorale prelude	A piece of organ music based on a hymn tune
Coda (It)	An addition to the last part of a piece of movement, to bring it to a satisfying end
Col, coll', colla (It)	With. Thus, *colla voce* (or *parte*) = the accompaniment to follow the solo voice or instrument

Coll' ottava (It)	With the octave (above or below)
Colla destra (It)	With the right hand
Colla sinistra (It)	With the left hand
Comodo (It)	Convenient; *tempo comodo* = at a convenient speed (neither too fast or too slow)
Con (It)	With
Con anima (It)	With life
Con brio (It)	With vivacity, spirit
Con espressione (It)	With expression
Con fuoco (It)	With fire
Con grazia (It)	With grace
Con moto (It)	With motion
Con spirito (It)	With spirit
Concerto	In the 17th and early 18th centuries the *concerto grosso* was an orchestral work in several movements, in which passages for a small group of instruments (*concertino*) are contrasted with *tutti* passages played by the full orchestra (*concerto grosso*). By the late 18th century the solo concerto, for one or more solo instruments with orchestra, had become established. The three movements were similar to those of a sonata, but without the Minuet and Trio. The first movement usually included a *cadenza*, in which the soloist was expected to improvise a virtuoso passage based on themes already heard. In later concertos the cadenza, instead of being improvised, was usually written into the movement by the composer, or by some other composer or performer
Counterpoint	(Lat. *punctus contre punctus* = note against note.) The combination of two or more independent parts or voices, each with its own melodic and rhythmic interest, to form a harmonious whole. Counterpoint in which two parts may be interchanged (inverted) is known as *double counterpoint*. If three parts may be interchanged it is known as *triple counterpoint*, and so on.
Courante (Fr)	(a) An Italian dance with 'running' figures,

generally in lively $\frac{3}{8}$ or $\frac{3}{4}$ time; (b) A French dance in rather slow $\frac{3}{2}$ or $\frac{6}{4}$ time

Crescendo (It)	Becoming louder (<)
Da capo (It)	From the beginning
Dal segno (It)	From the sign $
Decrescendo (It)	Becoming softer (>)
Delicato (It)	Delicate, gentle
Diminuendo (It)	Becoming softer
Dolente (It)	Sad
Doppio movimento (It)	Twice as fast
Douce (Fr), Dolce (It)	Sweet
E (It)	And
Ein (Ger)	One, a, an
Einfach (Ger)	Simple
En dehors (Fr)	*lit.* 'outside' – let one part stand out from the rest
Energico (It)	Energetic, vigorous
Espressivo (It)	Expressively
Etude (Fr)	Study
Facile (It)	Easy
Fine (It)	The end
Forte (It)	Loud
Forte-piano (It)	Loud, then soft
Fortissimo (It)	Very loud
Forza (It)	Force
Forzando; forzato (It)	Strongly accented
Frölich (Ger)	Cheerful, merry
Fugue	A contrapuntal piece in two or more parts, or *voices*, which may be divided into three sections: (a) *exposition*, with the voices entering in turn with the same theme (first in the tonic key (*subject*), then in the dominant (*answer*); (b) *middle section*, in which the entries appear in other keys, and may be linked by *episodes* (contrasting passages); (c) *final section*, in which the subject returns to the tonic key. A fugue may contain a *countersubject* (a melody combined in counterpoint with the subject), and many devices may be used during the course of a fugue, such as *augmentation*

and *diminution* (notes in double, or smaller, value than those of the original theme), *stretto* (in which the entries of the subject are brought closer together by overlapping), and *pedal-point* (*see* page 168). A fugue with two subjects, which may occur together or separately before being combined, is known as a *double fugue*

Furioso (It)	With fury, passion
Gavotte	A French dance in moderate $\frac{4}{4}$ time, usually starting at the half-bar
Gigue (Fr), Jig (Eng)	A lively dance, usually in $\frac{3}{8}$, $\frac{6}{4}$, $\frac{9}{8}$ or $\frac{12}{8}$ time, sometimes with a fugal opening
Giocoso (It)	Joyful
Giusto (It)	Exact, reasonable
Glissando (It)	Sliding
Grandioso (It)	Grand, magnificent
Grave (It)	Solemn, slow
Grazioso (It)	Graceful
Humoreske (Ger)	A piece of capricious character
Imitation	A contrapuntal device in which a melodic theme is restated in different parts or voices, and at different pitches
Incalzando (It)	Hastening
Lacrimosa (It)	Sad
Langsam (Ger)	Slow
Largamente (It)	Broadly
Larghetto (It)	Slow, but less slow than *largo*
Largo (It)	Broad, slow
Legato (It)	Smooth
Legéremènt (Fr)	Lightly, nimbly
Leggiero (It)	Lightly
Leitmotiv (Ger)	*See* page 187
Lento (It)	Slow
Lied (Ger)	Song
L'istesso tempo (It)	The same time
Loure (Fr)	A slow dance in $\frac{6}{4}$ or $\frac{3}{4}$ time (used in Bach's *Fifth French Suite*)
Lunga pausa (It)	Long pause
Lusingando (It)	Coaxing, caressing

Ma (It)	But
Madrigal	A musical setting of a poem for unaccompanied voices in several parts, often in imitative style
Maestoso (It)	Majestic
Maggiore (It)	Major
Main droite (Fr)	Right hand
Main gauche (Fr)	Left hand
Mano destra (It)	Right hand
Mano sinistra (It)	Left hand
Marcato (It)	Marked
Marziale (It)	Martial
Mass	A choral setting of the Ordinary, or invariable, parts of the mass, i.e. *Kyrie, Gloria, Credo, Sanctus* with *Benedictus, Agnus Dei.* Masses have been written by many composers such as Palestrina, Byrd and Bach. *Requiem* masses for the dead have been written by Mozart, Berlioz, Verdi, Fauré and others
Meno mosso (It)	Less movement
Mesto (It)	Sad
Mezzo forte (It)	Moderately loud
Mezzo piano (It)	Moderately soft
Minuet	A French dance in moderate $\frac{3}{4}$ time. It became a regular movement in the classical sonata and symphony, in ternary form (minuet-trio-minuet)
Misura (It)	Measure (bar). Thus, *alla misura*, in strict time
Mit (Ger)	With
Molto (It)	Much
Morendo (It)	Dying away
Motet	A short choral setting of a sacred Latin text, usually in contrapuntal style, and unaccompanied
Niente (It)	Nothing
Nobilmente (It)	Nobly
Non troppo (It)	Not too much
Ohne (Ger)	Without
Ossia (It)	Or. Used to indicate an alternative passage

Ostinato (It)	A theme or figure which is continually repeated during a section, or the whole, of a composition. If it occurs in the bass it is called *ground bass*
Overture	In the classical period the overture was usually the introductory music to an opera, oratorio, play, etc. In the 17th and 18th centuries overtures were of two types: (1) French, established by Lulli, consisting of a slow movement, quick movement in imitative style, and sometimes a final dance movement (minuet or gavotte); (2) Italian, consisting of a quick movement followed by a slow movement, and ending with a quick movement. From the 19th century *concert* overtures were written as independent pieces (e.g. Mendelssohn, *Calm Sea* and *Prosperous Voyage*, 1828)
Partita	Used by Bach and others in the sense of 'suite' (q.v.)
Passacaglia (It)	Originally a dance form, but later a piece in which a melodic bass theme is continually repeated while the treatment of the other parts is varied
Passepied (Fr)	A lively dance in $\frac{3}{8}$ or $\frac{6}{8}$ time
Pastorale (It)	In a pastoral style
Perdendosi (It)	Gradually dying away
Pesante (It)	Heavy
Piacevolo (It)	In a pleasant manner
Pianissimo (It)	Very soft
Piano (It)	Soft
Più mosso (It)	More movement
Plainsong (Plainchant)	The style of unison singing established by Pope Gregory (*c.* 540–604), based on the old church modes (*see* page 33), and often called *Gregorian Chant*
Pochettino (It)	Very little
Polonaise (Fr)	A Polish dance in moderately fast $\frac{3}{4}$ time, with a rhythm such as

	the phrases usually end on the last beat of the bar
Polyrhythm	The simultaneous use of two or more different rhythms in different parts (e.g. piano: three notes in the right hand against five in the left)
Portamento (It)	Gliding from one note to the next
Prelude	A short instrumental or orchestral piece, for example Chopin *Preludes* for piano (1839), Debussy *Prélude à l'aprés-midi d'un faune* for orchestra (1894). Also a short introduction to an opera, etc. (e.g. Wagner *Prelude to Lohengrin* (1850))
Prestissimo (It)	As quick as possible
Presto (It)	Quick, lively
Programme music	*See* footnote on page 187
Quasi (It)	As if
Quartet	A composition for four performers (instrumental or vocal); a string quartet is for two violins, viola and cello. Other instrumental combinations, with or without piano, are trio for three performers, and quintet, sextet, septet, octet and nonet, for five, six, seven, eight and nine performers
Ralentir (Fr)	Slacken speed
Rallentando (It)	Gradually becoming slower
Recitative	A free style of singing, much used in early opera and oratorio. It is more related to dramatic speech than to song, and is accompanied by continuo chords (*secco*) or by the orchestra (*stromentato*)
Retenu (Fr)	Hold back speed
Rhapsody	An instrumental piece in a free, rhapsodic style
Rinforzando (It)	*Lit.* 'reinforcing' – a sudden strong accent on a note or chord
Risoluto (It)	Resolute
Ritardando (It)	Gradually becoming slower
Ritenuto (It)	Held back
Rondo	*Simple rondo* consists of one principal

theme which recurs at least three times, but which alternates with different sections, or *episodes*. The form may therefore be *ABACADA* etc. *Sonata-rondo*, sometimes used by Beethoven and others for the last movement of a sonata, is a combination of rondo and sonata form. In the exposition, the codetta is replaced by a return to the first subject in the tonic key. Since the first section is complete, the middle section usually consists of new material (*episode*) in a new key. In the recapitulation, instead of the codetta there is a final appearance of the first subject

Round	*See* canon
Rubato (It)	*See* tempo rubato
Ruhig (Ger)	Peaceful
Sans (Fr)	Without
Sarabande (Fr)	An expressive piece in slow $\frac{3}{2}$ or $\frac{3}{4}$ time, with a pronounced accent on the second beat of the bar e.g. $\frac{3}{4}$ ♩♩ ♩ or ♪♩♩ ♩)
Scherzando (It)	Playfully
Scherzo (It)	*Lit.* 'joke'. After 1750 usually in quick $\frac{3}{4}$ time, often replacing the minuet as a movement in a sonata or symphony
Schnell (Ger)	Quick
Seconda (It)	Second
Segue (It)	Follow on without a break; continue pattern of notes or chords
Sehr (Ger)	Very
Semplice (It)	In a simple manner
Sempre (It)	Always
Senza (It)	Without
Sequence	The repetition of a melodic or harmonic pattern at a different pitch
Sforzando; sforzato (It)	Strongly accented
Siciliano (It)	A Sicilian dance in moderately slow $\frac{6}{8}$ or $\frac{12}{8}$ time, usually with a dotted rhythm such as $\frac{6}{8}$ ♩. ♪♪ ♪♪♪ |

Simile (It)	Similar; used when a pattern of phrasing, etc. is to be continued
Smorzando (It)	Dying away
Sonata	Originally an instrumental piece, as opposed to *cantata*, a piece for voices. After 1750, a composition in several movements for one or two instruments. A short sonata, usually elementary, is called a *sonatina*
Sonata form	A term for the form often used since 1750 for the first movement (and sometimes other movements) of a sonata, string quartet, symphony, etc. Sonata form is made up of three sections, which may be preceded by an introduction: *exposition*, *development* and *recapitulation*.

The exposition consists of a theme called the *first subject* in the tonic key, and a contrasted theme called the *second subject* usually in the key of the dominant or relative major. The two subjects may be linked together by a *bridge passage*, or *transition*. The closing section, or *codetta*, is in the key of the second subject, and may consist of new material.

In the development, the two themes may be introduced in various keys, and developed by discursive means (new harmonization or accompaniment, imitative or contrapuntal devices, etc.).

In the recapitulation, the first subject reappears in the tonic key, leading to the second subject, also in the tonic key. After the codetta in the tonic key, the movement often ends with a *coda* to bring it to a satisfactory conclusion

Sonoro (It)	Sonorous
Sopra (It)	Above
Sostenuto (It)	Sustained
Sotto (It)	Below. Thus, *sotto voce*, in an undertone, softly
Staccato (It)	Detached

Stringendo (It) Increasing the speed

Suite Before 1750 the suite consisted of a group of dance movements in the same key. Later, in the hands of Bach and his contemporaries, the basic dances consisted of the allemande, courante, sarabande and gigue, in that order; one or more other dances, such as the bourrée, gavotte, minuet or passepied, were added, usually after the sarabande. In the 19th century the word 'suite' was used for any group of instrumental pieces, often drawn from ballet, etc.

Symphony Since *c.* 1750 the word 'symphony' has been used in the sense of a sonata for orchestra

Tempo (It) Time

Tempo giusto (It) In exact time

Tempo primo (It) At the original speed

Tempo rubato (It) *Lit.* 'in robbed time', in other words a time in which one part of a bar is played slower or faster at the expense of the other part.

Teneramente (It) Tenderly

Tenuto (It) Held, sustained

Tierce de Picardy (Fr) The use of the major 3rd in the tonic chord at the end of a piece in a minor key; found extensively in music composed between *c.* 1500 and 1750

Toccata A piece for a keyboard instrument, designed to display the dexterity of the performer

Tranquillo (It) Tranquil, peaceful

Tre corde (It) Three strings (i.e. release the left piano pedal)

Tremolo (It) The rapid reiteration of one or more notes. On stringed instruments, bowed *tremolo* is obtained by rapid movements of the bow on a single note or chord, written thus

and fingered *tremolo* by the rapid
alternation of two notes written

A similar finger *tremolo* may be obtained on
the piano

Tres (Fr)	Very
Triste (It)	Sad
Troppo (It)	Too much
Tutti (It)	All parts or performers
Una corda (It)	One string (i.e. depress the left piano pedal)
Und (Ger)	And
Variations	A form in which a theme is announced, and then repeated with modifications, by varying the melody, harmony, rhythm, texture, etc. From the late 18th century variations have been written as a movement in a sonata, etc. (e.g. Beethoven, *Sonata in F minor*, Op. 57, 1804–5), or as a complete work (e.g. Elgar, *Enigma Variations*, 1899)
Veloce (It)	Quick
Vif (Fr)	Lively
Vivace (It)	Lively, brisk
Vivo (It)	Animated
Volante (It)	*Lit.* 'flying', fast and light
Volta (It)	Time. Thus, *primo volta*, first time
Volti subito (It)	Turn over quickly
Wenig (Ger)	Little
Zart (Ger)	To, too, for
Zwei (Ger)	Two

REFERENCE LIST OF INSTRUMENTS AND ORCHESTRAL TERMS IN FOUR LANGUAGES

(Abbreviations and alternatives are shown in brackets.)

English	Italian	French	German
Bass Clarinet (B.Cl.)	Clarinetto basso (or Clarone) (Cl.b., or Cl.ne)	Clarinette basse (Clar. b.)	Bassklarinette (Bskl.)
Bass Drum (B.D.)	Gran Cassa (G.C.)	Grosse Caisse (G.C.)	Grosse Trommel (gr. Tr.)
Bass Flute (Bs. Fl.)	Flauto basso (Fl. basso)	Flûte Basse (Fl. Basse)	Bassflöte (Basfl.)
Bassoon (Bsn.)	Fagotto (Fag.)	Basson (Bn.)	Fagott (Fg.)
Bass Trumpet (Bs. Trpt.)	Tromba bass (Trb. bass)	Trompette basse (Tr. Basse)	Basstrompete (Basstrp.)
Bell up (Horn)	campana in aria	pavillon en l'air	schalltrichter auf
Bells	Campane (or Campanelle)	Cloches	Glocken
Brassy (Horn)	chiuso	cuivré	schmetternd
Castanets (Casts.)	Castagnette (Cast.)	Catagnettes (Cast.)	Kastagnetten (Kast.)
Celesta (Cel.)	Celeste (Cel.)	Célesta (Cel.)	Celeste (Cel.)
Clarinet (Cl.)	Clarinetto (Cl.)	Clarinette (Clr.)	Klarinette (Kl.)
Cornet (Cor.)	Cornetto a pistoni (Cor. a p.)	Cornet-à-pistons (C. a p. or Pn.)	Cornett (Cor.)

English	Italian	French	German
Cymbals (Cym.)	Piatti (or Cinelli) (Piat. or Cin.)	Cymbales (Cym.)	Becken (Beck.)
Desk	leggio	pupitre	Pult
Divided (Div.)	divisi (div.)	divisé (div.)	getheilt (get.)
Double Bass (or Bass) (Db. or Bs.)	Contrabasso (Cb.)	Contrebasse (C.b.)	Kontrabass (Kb.)
Double Bassoon (D. Bsn.)	Contrafagotto (C. Fag.)	Contre Basson (C. Bn.)	Kontrafagott (Kfg.)
English Horn (E.H.)	Corno Inglese (C. Ing.)	Cor Anglais (Cor. Ang.)	Englisches Horn (Engl. Hn.)
Euphonium (Euph.)	Euphonie (Euph.)	Euphonion (Euph.)	Euphonion (Euph.)
Flugel Horn (Flugel)	Flicorno (Flic.)	Bugle	Flugelhorn
Flute (Fl.)	Flauto (Fl.)	Flûte (Fl.)	Flöte (Fl.)
Full Score	Partitura	Partition	Partitur
Glockenspiel (Glock.)	Campanelli (or Campanetta) (Cmplli. or Camptta.)	Carillon (or Jeu de Timbres) (Car.)	Glockenspiel (Gloksp.)
Gong (G.)	Tam-tam (T-t)	Tam-tam (T-t)	Tam-tam (T-t)
Harp (Hp.)	Arpa (Arp.)	Harpe (Hrp.)	Harfe (Hrf.)
Hammered	martellato	martelé	markiert
Horn (Hn.)	Corno (Cor.)	Cor	Horn (Hrn.)
Kettledrums (or Timpani) (Timp.)	Timpani (Timp.)	Timbales (Timb.)	Pauken (Pk.)
Muted	con sordino (con. sord.)	avec sourdine	mit dämpfer (m. d.) (or gedämpft - for Horns)
Oboe (Ob.)	Oboe (Ob.)	Hautbois (Hb.)	Hoboe (or Oboe) (Hob. or Ob.)
Oboe d'amore (Ob. d'amore)	Oboe d'amore (Ob. d'am)	Hautbois d'amore (Hb. d'amore)	Oboe d'amore (Ob. d'amore)
On (near) the bridge	sul ponticello	sur le chevalet	zum Steg
On the fingerboard	sul tasto (or flautato)	sur la touche	am griffbrett
Open	aperto (i)	ouvert(s)	offen
Percussion	Percussione	Batterie	Schlagzeug
Piccolo (Picc.)	Flauto Piccolo (or Ottavino) (Fl. Picc. or Ott.)	Petite Flûte (Pte. Flt.)	Kleine Flöte (Kl. Fl.)

English	*Italian*	*French*	*German*
Rattle (or Ratchet)	Raganella (Rg.)	Crécelle	Klapper (or Ratsche)
Roll	rollo	roulement	wirbel
Saxophone (Sax.)	Sassofone (Sassof.)	Saxophone (Sax.)	Saxophon (Sax.)
Side Drum (or Snare Drum) (S.D.)	Tamburo Militarie (T.M.)	Tambour Militaire (or Caisse claire) (Tamb. or C.Cl.)	Kleine Trommel (kl. Tr.)
Stopped (Horn)	chiuso	bouché	gestopft
String	corda	corde	Saite
Tabor (Tab.)	Tamburo (Tamb.)	Tambourin (or Tambour de Provence) (T. de P.)	Tambourin (Tamb.)
Tambourine (Tamb.)	Tamburino (Tambrno.)	Tambour de Basque (T. de B.)	Schellentrommel (Schell.)
Tenor Drum (T.D.)	Tamburo rullante (Tamb. r.)	Caisse roulante (Caisse r.)	Rührtrommel (R. tr.)
Triangle (Trgl.)	Triangolo (Trgl.)	Triangle (Trg.)	Triangel (Trgl.)
Trombone (Trb.)	Trombone (Trb.)	Trombone (Trb.)	Posaune (Pos.)
Trumpet (Tpt.)	Tromba (Tr.)	Trompette (Trp)	Trompete (Trp.)
Tuba (Tb.)	Tuba (Tb.)	Tuba (Tb.)	Tuba (or Basstuba) (Tb. or Bt.)
Unison (Unis.)	unisono (unis.)	unies	zusammen (or einfach)
Unmuted	senza sordino (senza sord.)	sans sourdine (sans sourd.)	ohne dämpfer
Valve Horn	Corno Ventile	Cor-à-pistons	Ventilhorn
Valve Trumpet	Tromba Ventile	Trompette-à-pistons	Ventiltrompete
Viola (Vla.)	Viola (Vla.)	Alto (Alt.)	Bratsche (Br.)
Violin (Vln.)	Violino (Viol.)	Violon (Von.)	Violine (or Geige) (Viol.)
Violoncello (Cello or Vlc.)	Violoncello (Vc.)	Violoncelle (Vc.)	Violoncell (Vcl.)
With the back of the bow	col legno (ligno)	avec le bois	col legno (or mit Holz)
With the bow	coll' arco	avec l'archet	mit Bogen
Xylophone (Xyl.)	Silafano (Silf.)	Xylophone (Xyloph.)	Xylophon (Xyl.)

CHECKLIST OF COMPOSERS

Early music (*c.* 1550–1750)

Tallis, Thomas
(English)
(*c.* 1505–85)

Gabrieli, Andrea
(Italian)
(*c.* 1510–86)

Palestrina, Giovanni
(Italian)
(*c.* 1525–94)

Lassus, Roland de
(Dutch)
(1532–94)

Byrd, William
(English)
(1543–1623)

Gabrieli, Giovanni
(Italian)
(1555–1612)

Monteverdi, Claudio
(Italian)
(1567–1643)

Tomkins, Thomas
(English)
(1572–1656)

Wilbye, John
(English)
(1574–1638)

Weelkes, Thomas
(English)
(*c.* 1576–1623)

Gibbons, Orlando
(English)
(1583–1625)

Frescobaldi, Girolamo
(Italian)
(1583–1643)

Corelli, Arcangelo
(Italian)
(1653–1713)

Purcell, Henry
(English)
(1659–95)

Scarlatti, Alessandro
(Italian)
(1660–1725)

Couperin, François
('Le Grand')
(French)
(1668–1733)

Vivaldi, Antonio
(Italian)
(1675–1741)

Telemann, Georg Philipp
(German)
(1681–1767)

Morley, Thomas
(English)
(1557–*c.* 1602)

Sweelinck, Jan
Pieterszoon
(Dutch)
(1562–1621)

Dowland, John
(English)
(1563–1626)

Bull, John
(English)
(1563–1628)

Farnaby, Giles
(English)
(*c.* 1566–1640)

Schütz, Heinrich
(German)
(1585–1672)

Cavalli, Pietro
(Italian)
(1602–76)

Lully, Jean-Baptiste
(French)
(1632–87)

Blow, John
(English)
(1649–1708)

Pachelbel, Johann
(German)
(1653–1706)

Rameau, Jean Philippe
(French)
(1683–1764)

Bach, Johann Sebastian
(German)
(1685–1750)

Scarlatti, Domenico
(Italian)
(1685–1757)

Handel, George Frideric
(German)
(1685–1759)

Gluck, Christoph
(German)
(1714–87)

—— Classical music (*c.* 1750–1825) ——

Haydn, Joseph
(Austrian)
(1732–1809)

Mozart, Wolfgang
Amadeus
(Austrian)
(1756–91)

Beethoven, Ludwig van
(German)
(1770–1827)

_____ Early Romantic music _____
(*c.* 1825–1850)

Weber, Carl Maria von
(German)
(1786–1826)

Meyerbeer, Giacomo
(German)
(1791–1864)

Schubert, Franz
(Austrian)
(1797–1828)

Berlioz, Hector
(French)
(1803–69)

Mendelssohn
(Bartholdy), Felix
(German)
(1809–47)

Chopin, Frédéric
(Polish)
(1810–49)

Rossini, Gioacchino
(Italian)
(1792–1868)

Glinka, Mikhail
(Russian)
(1804–57)

Schumann, Robert
(German)
(1810–56)

Late Romantic music (c. 1850–1900)

Liszt, Franz
(Hungarian)
(1811–86)

Wagner, Richard
(German)
(1813–83)

Verdi, Giuseppe
(Italian)
(1813–1901)

Offenbach, Jacques
(German–French)
(1819–80)

Franck, César
(Belgian)
(1822–90)

Smetana, Bedřich
(Czech)
(1824–84)

Bruckner, Anton
(Austrian)
(1824–96)

Strauss, Johann (the younger)
(Austrian)
(1825–99)

Borodin, Alexander
(Russian)
(1833–87)

Brahms, Johannes
(German)
(1833–87)

Bizet, Georges
(French)
(1838–75)

Mussorgsky, Modest
(Russian)
(1839–81)

Tchaikovsky, Peter Ilyich
(Russian)
(1840–93)

Dvořák, Antonin
(Czech)
(1841–1904)

Sullivan, Sir Arthur
(English)
(1842–1900)

Grieg, Edvard
(Norwegian)
(1843–1907)

Rimsky-Korsakov, Nikolay
(Russian)
(1844–1908)

The Modern Age (c. 1900–)

Saint-Saëns, Charles
(French)
(1835–1921)

Sibelius, Jean
(Finnish)
(1865–1957)

Kodály, Zoltán
(Hungarian)
(1882–1967)

Balakirev, Mily
(Russian)
(1837–1910)

Fauré, Gabriel
(French)
(1845–1924)

Elgar, Sir Edward
(English)
(1857–1934)

Puccini, Giacomo
(Italian)
(1858–1924)

Mahler, Gustav
(Austrian)
(1860–1911)

Debussy, Claude
(French)
(1862–1918)

Delius, Frederick
(English)
(1862–1934)

Strauss, Richard
(German)
(1864–1949)

Falla, Manuel de
(Spanish)
(1876–1946)

Bartók, Béla
(Hungarian)
(1881–1945)

Gershwin, George
(American)
(1898–1937)

Poulenc, Francis
(French)
(1899–1963)

Satie, Erik
(French)
(1866–1925)

Vaughan Williams,
Ralph
(English)
(1872–1958)

Rachmaninov, Sergey
(Russian)
(1873–1943)

Holst, Gustav
(English)
(1874–1934)

Schoenberg, Arnold
(Austrian)
(1874–1951)

Ravel, Maurice
(French)
(1875–1937)

Walton, Sir William
(English)
(1902–83)

Tippett, Sir Michael
(English)
(1905–)

Shostakovitch, Dmitri
(Russian)
(1906–75)

Messiaen, Olivier
(French)
(1908–)

Cage, John
(American)
(1912–)

Britten, Benjamin
(English)
(1913–76)

Stravinsky, Igor
(Russian)
(1882–1971)

Webern, Anton von
(Austrian)
(1883–1945)

Berg, Alban
(Austrian)
(1885–1935)

Varèse, Edgard
(French)
(1885–1965)

Prokofiev, Sergey
(Russian)
(1891–1953)

Hindemith, Paul
(German)
(1895–1963)

Ligeti, György
(Hungarian)
(1923–)

Boulez, Pierre
(French)
(1925–)

Berio, Luciano
(Italian)
(1925–)

Henze, Hans Werner
(German)
(1926–)

Stockhausen, Karlheinz
(German)
(1928–)

Penderecki, Krzysztof
(Polish)
(1933–)

Copland, Aaron
(American)
(1900–90)

Bernstein, Leonard
(American)
(1918–90)

Birtwistle, Sir Harrison
(English)
(1934–)

Davies, Peter Maxwell
(English)
(1934–)

ANSWERS TO
—— SELF-TESTING ——
QUESTIONS

3   (a) Minor 6th; (b) Minor 3rd; (c) Perfect 5th; (d) Augmented 4th.

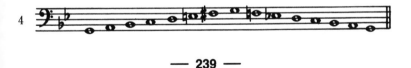

Page 128

2 (a) Plucked with the finger.
   (b) Muted.
   (c) A small piece of horn, ivory, etc. used to pluck the string of instruments like the guitar.
   (d) A method of articulating rapid passages on the flute, etc.
   (e) An orchestral horn in F which can be switched to a higher B flat section.
   (f) Single-headed bass drum.

3 Oboe, bassoon, heckelphone, bass oboe.

4 C flat.

5 Sopranino, descant, treble, tenor, bass.

6 Timpani, or kettledrums.

7 Viola, cello.

8 Saxophone.

Page 173

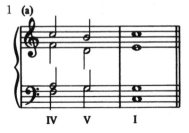

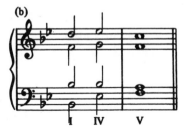

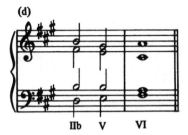

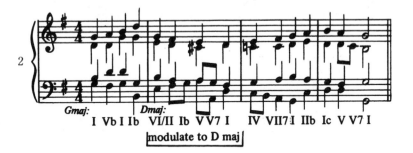

———————— **Page 217** ————————

1   Pope Gregory I; Gregorian Chant.

2   Alessandro Scarlatti.

3   J. S. Bach and Handel.

4   (a)   J. S. Bach   (l)   Stravinsky
    (b)   Haydn   (m) Debussy
    (c)   Beethoven   (n)   Richard Strauss
    (d)   Schumann   (o)   Vaughan Williams
    (e)   Berlioz   (p)   Schoenberg
    (f)   Sibelius   (q)   Prokofiev
    (g)   Verdi   (r)   Ravel
    (h)   Wagner   (s)   Bartók
    (i)   Johann Strauss the younger   (t)   Walton
    (j)   Mussorgsky   (u)   Britten
    (k)   Sullivan   (v)   Penderecki

5   In the negro quarters of New Orleans, towards the beginning of the twentieth
    century.

SUGGESTIONS FOR FURTHER STUDY

The AB Guide to Music Theory, Taylor, Parts 1 and 2 (Associated Board)
Music Theory in Practice, Taylor, Grades 1 to 8 (Associated Board)
These books are based on the theory syllabus of the Associated Board

The Cambridge Music Guide, Sadie & Latham (Cambridge University Press)
The Concise Oxford History of Music, Abraham (Oxford University Press)
A Companion to the Orchestra, Del Mar (Faber)
The Faber Companion to 20th-Century Popular Music, Hardy & Laing (Faber)
The Oxford Companion to Popular Music, Gammond (Oxford University Press)
Popular Music of the Non-Western World, Manuel (Oxford University Press)
Dictionary of Composers and Their Music, Gilder (Sphere Music)
Electronic and Computer Music, Manning (Oxford University Press)
What's a Synthesizer?, Eiche (Faber)
Teach Yourself The Piano, Palmer (Hodder & Stoughton) (Book/cassette pack also available)
Six Violin Lessons with Yehudi Menuhin (Faber)
Instrumental Technique series (Oxford University Press). Titles include:
 Recorder (Rowland-Jones), *Clarinet* (Thurston), *Oboe* (Rothwell), *Trumpet* (Dale), *Trombone* (Wick), *Guitar* (Quine)
Sing, Clap and Play Keyboard, Rickard & Cox (Oxford University Press)

INDEX